Broken Boys Become Broken Men

Shon Y. Hart

BROKEN BOYS

Become

BROKEN MEN

The Journey of Becoming Whole

SHON Y. HART

BROKEN BOYS BECOME BROKEN MEN

Scriptures noted NIV are taken from the Holy Bible: New International Version®. Copyright © 1973, 1978, 1984 by International Bible Society.
Scriptures noted NKJV are taken from New King James Version. Copyright © 1979, 1980, 1982, Thomas Nelson, Inc., Publishers.

Editorial Supervision: Jody Sedrick, Leah Hart, Shelby Hart
Cover designs/ artwork: Joshua Wirth
Photography: Leni Kai

Ordering Information:
Quantity sales. Special discounts are available on quantity purchases by corporations, associations, and others. For details, contact the publisher at the address below.

LiveInspired
P.O. Box 703
Flint, MI 48501
313-757-1388
shonhart@involveddad.org
www.shonhart.com

ISBN- 9798399183329
ISBN-
Printed in the United States of America

DEDICATION

This book is dedicated to my incredible family and to the men I have had the honor to serve at InvolvedDad.

Firstly, to God, who has gifted me with the ability to impact the lives of those He assigned to me. I would also like to thank Him for opening doors of opportunity and using me as a living vessel.

To my dear children, Sydni, Shelby, and Levi, I want to express my heartfelt gratitude to God for your presence in my life. I hope this book will testify to my affection for you and a record of my thoughts that will endure beyond my time on earth. I want this to offer you a glimpse into who I was and what I stood for and to serve as a meaningful legacy for you and the future generations of our family, including my grandchildren yet to come.

To Leah, my wonderful life partner and the constant pillar of support - your inspiration has driven me to strive for greatness in every aspect of my life. Your unyielding faith in me has been my fortress, always making me feel as if I were royalty in your eyes. This empowering emotion propelled me, providing the bravery and motivation to see this journey through. Thank you, my shining star, for everything you've contributed.

To my father, who has inspired me to continue to grow. I love you so much, Dad. What was once embedded in pain is not loathed in love. Thank you, Dad, for everything.

Finally, yet significantly, this book is devoted to the remarkable men I've had the honor of serving at InvolvedDad. Your tenacity and resolve to evolve have consistently inspired me. You've imparted priceless wisdom about fortitude, tenacity, and the potential for personal metamorphosis. Every hurdle you've encountered; each stride you've made toward self-betterment has energized my own path. My sincerest gratitude to you, gentlemen, for everything. I want you to understand that your narratives and experiences catalyze my relentless drive to make a difference every day, for each and every one of you.

FORWARD

Broken! To some extent, we are all broken. We don't like to admit that we are broken. We walk through life burying our pain, putting on a mask to show the world we have it all together, that we are in control, that we are masters of our own destiny. We wear the mask of bravery, positivity, and of confidence but the reality is the mask is just a façade hiding the real pain and disappointment of life's challenges. If we are honest with ourselves sometimes the mask, we wear is more for ourselves than for others.

It takes courage to admit that you're broken.
There is a principle of broken that permeates life. A principle that when embraced leads to the greatest growth. At the beginning of every harvest season for tills the ground. There is no harvest until the ground is broken which allows a seed to be planted. There is no plant until the seed is broken. In the dark cover of the heavy soil, the broken seedling works its way up until it finally breaks through the soil. One might think the journey is complete as the seedling becomes a plant, but a plant's purpose is to flower and bear fruit or grain. Once again, the plant is broken as the growing bud finally breaks revealing a flower that will break and begin the process of producing fruit which ultimately sustains life.

The challenge is we tend to revolt and fight against the principle of being broken. Similar to the weight and darkness of soil upon a seed, life's trials and tribulations can burden our spirits, leaving us feeling forsaken, desolate, and devoid of hope. However, as we embrace the dark moments of our life, we begin the profound process of growth and transformation where we discover that being broken is the first step to our becoming Unbroken.

My wife often reminds me that "You don't know the back story. So always extend grace and lead with love." This has become our family's mantra. You like no other know your back story. You may see yourself as broken and unredeemable but as you will see in this book being broken is part of the redeeming process, especially when coupled with grace, humility, and self-love. In this book, Shon exposes the reality and heartache of being broken — sharing very authentically his back story. He sheds light on the process of becoming, the struggle of working through, the challenge of watching your own film, wrestling with forgiveness, confronting self-doubt, authentically owning the good, bad, and ugly of the back story, learning to see through His eyes, and ultimately becoming Unbroken.

Shon's journey is a powerful testament and blueprint of the immense potential within each one of us when we embrace the reality of being broken, owning our story, and beginning the transformative path to becoming Unbroken.

Jody Sedrick
Host of Fathers Fire Podcast
Author of "Learn to Dance with The Currents of Life – When You Feel Like Drowning"

As a small boy, my father was everything to me - my best friend, and my superhero. If I could grow up to be even a fraction of the man he was, I thought, I would consider my life a success. Yet, as I transitioned into my teenage years, my perspective began to shift. My worldview expanded and the tight bond between my father and me started to loosen. As the pieces of life's puzzle fell into place, it became clear that my father, while always a constant presence, couldn't walk my journey into manhood for me. That was a path I had to tread alone.

By the time I had grown into a young adult, the gap between us had widened to a point of estrangement. The news of my parent's divorce after 28 years of marriage, though shocking, arrived at a time when I was wrestling with my own challenges as a young husband and father. I was in my early 20s, navigating the complex terrains of fatherhood, manhood, and family life with little to no guidance. Through sheer perseverance, I carved out an appearance of a successful life and raised a family, all while grappling with the wounds of a fractured childhood.

Those wounds bled into my interactions with older men, tinting my vision with skepticism and suspicion. I was perpetually on guard, subconsciously anticipating the discord of relationships as had happened with my father. But, with age comes wisdom, and after nearly 17 years of discontentment, my father and I have embarked on a journey of intentional healing, actively mending the tears in our relationship.

Through the lens of my own life experiences, coupled with open and honest conversations with him, I see my father as a superhero once more. Not because he's perfect or infallible, but because he is human. He is a man who did not have what he gave me - a present father. It is clear to me now that the patterns of brokenness repeat themselves, that broken boys often grow into broken men. The acknowledgment of this has been instrumental in reshaping my understanding of my father, and in turn, myself.

George E. Conway II

CONTENTS

Table Contents

INTRODUCTION

As a society, we frequently disregard and overlook the challenges young boys encounter as they mature. We tend to concentrate on the end goal of successful manhood, emphasizing qualities such as strength, independence, career achievements, and personal fulfillment. However, it's worth considering whether our definition of successful manhood is truly success at all. It's important to reflect on the boys who don't reach that level of achievement or the troubled boys who grow up to become struggling men. By extension, the result is we have a generation of struggling families because we've focused on successful manhood while neglecting the important aspect, and the desperate need for men who are good fathers as well.

As I delved into researching and preparing for this book, I stumbled upon some startling figures concerning father absenteeism. The U.S. Census Bureau reveals that a staggering 19.7 million kids, equating to more than 1 in 4, grow up without a father. Collected in 2021, this data highlights the pervasiveness of the issue and its impact on a significant portion of our society. Further studies by the National Fatherhood Initiative indicate that fatherless children are prone to encountering a host of challenges, such as higher poverty rates, behavioral problems, and academic struggles.

As an African American, I felt compelled to delve deeper, particularly into data related to men of color, specifically black men. The findings showed that black men are more susceptible to trauma, abandonment, bullying, neglect, and many other issues resulting in a lifetime of anguish and suffering than any other group. The American Psychological Association asserts that African American men are at a higher risk of falling victim to violent crime, enduring chronic health conditions, and facing poverty and unemployment. Look, this can be tough for any man to deal with. But when we are discussing how broken boys become broken men, it's stats like this that reveal how he can become broken. These adversities can also inflict long-lasting wounds that impede his mental and physical well-being, relationships, and chances of success.

Let me make this clear: this issue isn't exclusive to African American men. We will, however, examine and address the root causes that contribute to men of all races growing up fractured and broken. Men from every background face many challenges that can leave them feeling broken and disheartened, yet too ashamed to seek help. Pressures to conform to masculine stereotypes, stigmas surrounding mental health, judgments based on the car a man drives, the number of women he's been with, or the amount of money he makes—this list seems endless. Men are frequently discouraged from seeking the help and support they desperately need. This discouragement isn't always overt or in-your-face; at times, the subtle micro-aggressions deter men from reaching out for assistance. These micro-aggressions can reveal themselves in various ways, often unnoticed or dismissed by others. They may include making sarcastic comments about a man being sensitive, questioning a man's strength or toughness when he expresses vulnerability, or even making slick comments that imply he should "man up" or "not be a sissy." Ultimately, these examples may seem minuscule in the grand scheme of things. However, when this happens and accumulates over a long period, this can create an environment in which men feel discouraged from seeking help or expressing their true feelings, further perpetuating the cycle of emotional suppression and isolation.

When we think about the struggles that young boys face, it's important to understand that they are often expected to conform to narrow and rigid gender roles. Gender roles that hinder them from growing into whom they deserve to be and becoming. This can lead to toxic masculinity, a cultural norm that places a premium on stoicism, aggression, and dominance while suppressing emotions that reflect perceived "feminine" traits. Toxic masculinity can leave boys feeling isolated and refusing to seek help when they most desperately need it. In addition to displaying toxic masculinity traits, young boys can become angry due to the dismissal of their feelings and emotions with those they trust. A study published in the Journal of Interpersonal Violence found that men who experienced childhood neglect or abuse were likelier to report symptoms of depression, anxiety, and post-traumatic stress disorder (PTSD) in adulthood.

Reflecting on my experiences growing up in church, I vividly remember how people who showed signs of mental or emotional distress were often treated. The leaders and elders would attribute their struggles to demonic possession. Often, they would be encouraged to pray away their issues while the possibility that they might be dealing with a series of bad days, turmoil at home, job loss, or devastating news was dismissed. This left onlookers to conclude that they would not subject themselves to that and would rather suffer in silence. It's easy to see how this could make men hesitant to open up and deal with their emotions and problems publicly. Fearing that they would be looked at as weak or accused of colluding with the devil. So often, these men would retreat into their self-made caves of comfort and tend to their vices. Possible vices of alcoholism, sex addiction, aggression, pornography, shutting down emotionally, and/or running into the arms of another person, as they lacked a safe outlet to address their struggles.

Listen, I am not justifying these behaviors, however, I am telling you things I've learned to better understand how broken boys become broken men. Don't worry, when this journey is all over, I assure you that I will tell you how he can become free. I've personally walked this journey and know the weight of it and the liberating journey that awaits you. Believe me, if I can become free, anyone can.

In my teenage years, I remember the desperation of seeking my father's approval and validation. I say my teenage years, but to be completely honest I also sought his approval well into my adult life. But as a teenager, I was consumed with gaining my father's acceptance and approval. I did many things as a child to get his attention. Looking back, I realize that I would act out behaviorally, consciously, and unconsciously, just to get his attention. I'd misbehave even though I knew it might lead to a spanking or punishment—and trust me, his punishments were no joke. I remember this one time he put me on punishment just a few days into summer break, and I wasn't let off until a week or two before school started again. He claimed he'd forgotten he'd grounded me. Huh, yeah right, LOL! I can't say for sure if he did forget or not, but I do know I spent that entire summer indoors. I tell you, that was one long summer. Anyway, my freedom or desire to be freed from his captivity of not being seen became my motivating factor. I was willing to pay any price to break free from what I perceived to be his rejection of me and to be acknowledged by him.

My experiences with my dad reminded me of the emotions I experienced while watching the movie "Harriet." One scene, in particular, triggered back childhood memories and stirred intense feelings. In the movie, there's a heart-wrenching scene where Harriet confronts the slave owner, demanding the freedom promised to her and her family. She presents legal documentation as proof of their agreed-upon freedom, hoping that he would honor the binding contract. The slave master takes the document, scans it, and then lifts his head, his eyes filled with fury as he stares into their souls. In a crushing blow, he tears their freedom papers to shreds, banishes her husband, and threatens to kill him if he ever returns. Although our situations and the weight of each moment were vastly different, the results were personally devastating. This confrontation served as a catalyst for Harriet, igniting a fire within her to bring about change. It makes one ponder - would Harriet Tubman have risen to her legendary status had her slave master granted her the freedom she requested, rather than tearing up her freedom papers?

Maybe not, maybe she would have settled down with her husband and lived happily ever after." I often think about this and relate it to my own life. If I had not faced rejection and challenges, would I be who I am today? Would I have dedicated myself to restoring the bond between fathers and their children, advocating for systemic change? Honestly, the answer would be NO. Would you be who you are today if you did not experience what you have experienced? Reflect on that for a moment. Often, we seek relief or escape from uncomfortable situations, dreading the discomfort and pain they bring. Yet, when we grasp the transformative process of 'becoming,' our perspective on discomfort and pain shifts. Keep this thought close to your heart: it's not happening to me; it's happening for me. You need to know that you are right where you are and stop beating yourself up. Take this journey with me as we discover how and why broken boys become broken men and then embrace the journey to becoming unbroken.

-1-

INSTRUCTIONS NOT INCLUDED

"Instructions Not Included" is a phrase commonly seen on the packaging of DIY products. Sadly, it reflects the journey many boys embark upon as they transition from boyhood to manhood. As they navigate through each stage in the uncharted territory of becoming a man, they're bombarded with words and expectations to process alone. They hear phrases like, "Do it yourself, stop whining, stop complaining you sound like a girl, or stop crying before I give you something to cry about! You're acting like a girl!" These messages, filled with societal expectations and gender stereotypes, can create a confusing and isolating experience for young boys as they strive to define their identities and understand their roles in the world. This is the soundtrack of far too many children, and it hits differently when directed at boys.

Even though crying is a normal reaction to pain. The message pull yourself together; you're a boy, and boys don't cry over things like this.

We force boys to be silent. This message does more harm than good. When we tell boys to stay quiet, we unintentionally teach them to hide their feelings and emotions. This makes them think that their experiences don't matter, aren't normal, and should be suppressed and ignored. This way of thinking can cause long-term problems with boys' emotional health and ability to share their feelings. I know some people might handle things this way, and I've seen it happen many times. It's important to understand that this approach isn't helpful, especially if a young boy doesn't have an outlet. A well-intentioned mom might use this method to get her son ready for life's challenges. While she's doing her best to prepare her little boy for the tough world out there, she might not realize that her actions could unintentionally hurt his emotional growth and ability to not only talk about his feelings but embrace them positively.

A MOTHER'S ATTEMPT AT EMPOWERMENT

I can still recall when I was seven years old, and my mother made me confront a neighborhood bully. My friends and I were playing freeze tag, and the bully (we're gonna call him Tony), unable to catch me, grew increasingly frustrated. Every time he tried to tag me, I'd either dodge him or sprint past him making him look silly. The other kids would laugh, and his anger intensified. Eventually, he had enough of my shenanigans and punched me in the face. Pow, that was the sound of my face hitting Tony's hand. He then looked at me with confidence and said, "What is you going to do about it?" At that moment, I felt just like Red from the movie "Friday" after Debo took his bike. Tears streamed down my cheeks as I ran upstairs to find comfort from my mother. She was fed up with me constantly coming to her whenever something went wrong. I told her that Tony had hit me again, and she asked me why I wasn't outside fighting back. I said to myself, "What? What do you mean, why wasn't I outside fighting?"

I was truly afraid, and I didn't know how to tell her. While facing Tony filled me with fear, the greater concern was the perception of my mother and friends. How will they receive me if I were to lose or tell them that I was afraid? This is the perfect recipe for boys to clown other boys. On my block, you better have known how to fight or cap if not you were going to be the butt of everybody's jokes. Early on, I figured out the rules of the game - don't laugh too loud or too soft, and always laugh when the funny guy cracks a joke, or you're the next punchline. I just picked up how to dodge the bullets. Their words? They could cut right through you, no matter how tough you acted. Dripping with pure poison, those words could dig deep wounds that weren't quick to heal. The scars stuck around, a constant reminder of the soft spots hiding beneath the surface. On the outside, you'd act like you were made of stone, but inside, those words were trying to establish roots.

That age-old saying, "Sticks and stones may break my bones, but words will never hurt me," rings utterly false. Verbal attacks can leave wounds deeper and more lasting than any physical ones. Boys would brush off the words, putting on a tough exterior so that neither the girls nor their buddies could see the real pain and embarrassment hiding beneath. These moments serve as the first lessons in the art of mask-wearing for many young boys. In particular, it's the Hyena mask they slip on. Just like hyenas, they gather in groups, laughing and joking to distract from their inner turmoil. They rely on the strength of the pack to attack or to retreat. Since I never excelled at cracking jokes, my defense was to simply laugh along, a tactic to divert their attention and prevent them from turning their ridicule towards me. I didn't know if I was handling this situation right, so I did what I knew to do, become silent or laugh. What was I supposed to do? Was I supposed to just play it off as if it wasn't bothering me? Was I supposed to go and tell an adult? Was I supposed to stand there with a stone face with the intent to intimidate, or was I supposed to just sock him in the mouth? I didn't know, but what I wasn't going to do was let them know I was afraid. At the end of the day, there was no way I was going to tell them that I was afraid.

NAVIGATING CONFLICT AND EMOTIONS

In many of my presentations, I have encountered single mothers like my mom in the audience seeking advice for handling their young sons who face various challenges such as mine. These situations often involve a father who is either absent or inconsistently present, leading the young man to exhibit behaviors that the mother finds difficult to manage. She may struggle with the father's approach to teaching their son how to handle and resolve conflicts, which often involves aggression and domination. In such cases, she might be hesitant to intervene, fearing that she would be preventing the father from assuming his parental role. This experience sheds light on the challenges boys face when growing up without a comprehensive understanding of healthy masculinity.

My mother, with the best of intentions, tried to protect and empower me in an environment where societal norms and expectations surrounding masculinity often promoted unhealthy expressions. It is crucial to recognize that true manhood involves emotional intelligence, empathy, and constructive conflict resolution skills, rather than relying solely on aggression and violence. My mother was a good woman who navigated the complexities of raising a son in a difficult environment. Her love and dedication to my well-being were unwavering, and her actions were driven by her desire to see me succeed. She stepped into a role she didn't necessarily want to play due to my father's absence in handling these types of situations. She wanted me to learn to stand up for myself, particularly as a boy growing up in a tough neighborhood. Though I reluctantly managed to stand up to Tony, the experience left me with a lingering sense of confusion and conflicting emotions. I felt weak and I felt like I was punk. Despite having won the fight. My mother's involvement in pushing me to confront another boy added another layer of concern, leaving me questioning my own self-worth.

These unresolved questions remained with me, highlighting the need for clear guidance and support during boyhood. Many boys face similar challenges, often growing into men who struggle to navigate their own emotions and provide the necessary guidance to their sons. This cycle can continue, as these men may not have received the emotional support and instruction, they needed themselves.

In my life, I experienced the unique challenge of having a father who was physically present but emotionally distant. My mother tried her best to compensate for his emotional absence, providing the love and support I needed. However, the importance of emotional availability in parenting cannot be overstated, as it plays a crucial role in shaping a child's perspective and emotional well-being. The lingering impact of growing up with an emotionally distant father has shaped my perspective on parenthood and the importance of addressing the emotional well-being of my children. As I look back on my childhood, it's

11

clear to me now that my mother was doing the best, she could with what she had under the circumstances. She had to navigate the societal norms of the time and raise us with the resources available to her, all while dealing with the lack of emotional support and engagement from my father. This isn't to suggest that my father was completely absent, neglectful, or a deadbeat; he held up his duty as a provider, ensuring we had food on our table and clothes on our backs. However, the emotional aspect of fatherhood seemed to elude him.

My father was a hard worker, and his long hours meant that we only saw him sporadically during the day, and mostly at night. When he did come around, there wasn't much conversation or interaction. I remember feeling more fear than affection towards him, as he was the disciplinarian of the household. His interactions with us kids were marked by an absence of smiles and laughter. Oddly enough, he seemed more at ease, more vibrant, when interacting with his friends or children outside of our family. His approach to parenting was rooted in an old-school mindset that children should respect their elders, and he didn't believe in "playing" with children. It seemed to me that he was struggling with finding a balance between being a disciplinarian and offering nurturing support. I believe this struggle stemmed from his own upbringing, where he was likely not taught how to balance these aspects of fatherhood. His personal struggle manifested in his interactions with us, impacting our childhood experiences.

To break the cycle of emotional distance and promote healthy masculinity, it is essential to prioritize emotional availability and vulnerability in parenting. Fathers and father figures should be encouraged to connect with their sons on a deeper level, offering guidance and support during pivotal moments in their lives. Just recently, a man approached me, expressing his appreciation for the affectionate and engaged way I interacted with my son. To my son and me, our interaction was just that - normal. But I recognize that this isn't the norm for many. I'm consciously parenting my children, particularly my son, with the goal of fostering healthy emotional expression, vulnerability, resilience, accountability, and strength, among other values. This can help create a strong foundation for emotional well-being and resilience in boys as they grow into men. Equally important is the need for society to challenge and redefine traditional gender roles and expectations. Encouraging boys to express their emotions openly, seek help when needed, and engage in constructive conflict resolution can help create a new generation of emotionally intelligent men. This, in turn, will enable them to provide better support and guidance for their own children, breaking the cycle of emotional distance and unhealthy expressions of masculinity.

In my journey, I have made it my mission to promote emotional well-being and healthy masculinity through advocacy and education. By sharing my story, I hope to inspire others to recognize the importance of emotional availability and vulnerability in parenting and to challenge societal norms that perpetuate harmful stereotypes surrounding manhood. Only by addressing these issues head-on can we create lasting change for future generations of boys and men, empowering them to navigate the complexities of life with resilience, empathy, and emotional intelligence. It's essential to remember that everyone's journey is unique, and even without the guidance we might have hoped for, it's still possible to develop into a healthy, whole individual.

THE DANGER ZONE

When I first started my fatherhood program at InvolvedDad, there was this deeply moving moment during one of our early meetings. I saw a 60-year-old man we'll call John, a father of three, married for almost 40 years, and a respected community figure, break down in tears in another man's arms. He'd worked with teenagers, organized events to strengthen families, and was known for advocating justice. But there he was, openly weeping, sharing the pain of missing his own father's touch, wishing that when he was a kid, someone would have fought for justice for him. This gentleman had never confronted his own childhood trauma, caused by his verbally and physically abusive part-time father. Instead, he hid and suppressed his pain, all while raising a family, supporting his wife, and making a difference in his community. Sure, women face similar challenges, but they're often encouraged to seek help and talk about their feelings. Men, on the other hand, are told to hold back their tears, and if they cry, they're accused of acting like girls. As a little boy, John's pain came not just from enduring abuse, but also from being unable to rescue his mother from such violence. Witnessing his father's abuse towards his mother and feeling responsible for protecting her only intensified his sense of worthlessness. The heaviness of that emotional load was deeply etched into John's young heart. As he later started dating, fathering children, and eventually married, he approached love, affection, and parenting, inadvertently, through the lens of his own experiences.

I've seen it time and again, boys who grow up with absent or broken fathers or father figures tend to make vows of change. I understand this, but vows can be harmful. Most often, these young boys pledge never to resemble the father they had, or lacked, but are clueless about how to create a different behavior. Their life experiences become their

14

guide, forming the foundation of their decisions and actions. I can relate to this, yet I also believe that what we deliberately focus on, we become. If their minds are seared by images of neglect or trauma, there's a significant chance that they will echo that behavior. I personally needed to encounter something different to transform into something different. John's attention was on escaping the shadow of his father, rather than creating the picture of the father he aspired to be. He was resolute that he would never morph into his father and was adamant about breaking the cycle to be a better man for his own family.

This defense mechanism might have shielded him from mirroring his father's damaging patterns, but it also erected a wall between him, his wife, and his children. By neglecting to deal with his own trauma, wearing masks as a shield, and withdrawing into himself, John unintentionally made it challenging for his family to form an emotional bond with him. This hindered them from knowing his emotions and the struggles he might have been grappling with.

UNCOVERING THE IMPACT OF EMOTIONAL SHUTDOWN

Shutting down is a natural reaction for some men. Are you aware of when and if you shut down emotionally, either to escape, keep people out and away, or flat-out intimidate others? It's essential to recognize that even with the best of intentions, our efforts to overcome past trauma can sometimes lead to unforeseen challenges and repeating the same behavior, regardless of how badly we want to change. If you don't intentionally change, you won't change.

Maladaptive coping strategies are a scientific response to trauma aka destructive behaviors. Maladaptive coping strategies is a set of behaviors or strategies that people use to deal with stress or difficult emotions, but which ultimately are harmful or counterproductive. These coping mechanisms may provide temporary relief or distraction from the issue at hand, but they do not address the underlying problem and can often make the situation worse or create new problems. Our minds have the ability to establish memories and behaviors rooted in our experiences. These experiences turn into our way of life and our guideposts, causing us to imitate what we've been exposed to and consider it as the truth.

Destructive behaviors can show up in many different forms. It's a continuous journey of self-discovery and growth, where we learn to strike a balance between protecting ourselves and nurturing the relationships that matter most. As John peeled back layers of his journey, sharing his journey through that danger zone, he confessed how his loved ones—his wife and children—felt he was detached, uninterested in their emotional needs. They perceived him as being wrapped up in his own world. Isn't it interesting how those unresolved needs from childhood, those deeply seated traumas, and the defensive shields he built early in life, all came to the surface in his adult relationships? His family was in the dark, not realizing that the young boy, bruised and battered from his past, was still living inside the grown man they were dealing with daily. John, sculpted by fractured fatherhood, was misunderstood. But the thought that he didn't care or wasn't striving for his family's best was far from reality. Indeed, John cared with a depth that was difficult for him to express; he just didn't have the tools or the know-how to channel his feelings or tackle his own deeply embedded pain and trauma. His past experiences and coping strategies were barriers, preventing him from fully connecting with his loved ones.

Deep down inside, John desired to connect, but he was terrified to tap into that part of himself that was still afraid. That place was dark, unwelcoming, and not reassuring. He tried to avoid it with all his might, even though the wounded and broken boy inside desperately needed it and was screaming out for help. But the fear of letting go had a greater pull on him than his desire to be vulnerable and free. This narrative rings true for so many men today, their desire to be free and vulnerable gets overshadowed by the fear of letting go and facing the unknown. This was an ongoing battle within John, a struggle between his yearning to open up and his instinct to shield himself from rejection and pain. Sometimes, that struggle would leave him feeling lost and alone, even when he was in a room full of friends and loved ones.

John didn't become the man his father was, but he overcorrected and ended up on the opposite side of the tracks. No, he didn't abuse, assault, or abandon his family; instead, he emotionally abandoned them, becoming an extreme introvert who shut down his emotions. Some men really have a hard time identifying or processing their emotions; well, let me say some emotions. John confided in me that sometimes, to avoid getting hurt or causing more pain to others, he'd escape to his basement and indulge in his drug of choice or frequent the bar. He thought that he would find solace there, however, he found the total opposite. His escape would make him further isolate himself and unintentionally shut people out. As a young boy, John learned how to process his feelings by shutting down and keeping people out. It became his way of life. Left to experience and process everything alone, he arrived at his own conclusions. These coping habits had a lasting impact on his relationships, as he carried them into adulthood.

John's story highlights the importance of supporting boys when processing their emotions and experiences. Offering guidance and creating a safe space for them to express their feelings can help prevent the development of unhealthy coping mechanisms that may result in emotional disconnection later in life. By breaking the cycle of brokenness early, we can foster healthier relationships and build stronger families for future generations. When we allow children to interpret their experiences and draw conclusions without guidance, they often resort to coping mechanisms that are harmful rather than helpful. It's imperative to identify, address, and help our boys sidestep these maladaptive behaviors before they become entrenched, thereby disrupting the cycle of the wounded heart.

We have a responsibility to guide young boys in processing their traumas and fostering healthier thought patterns and coping strategies. Even though John was committed to being a better man than his father, he didn't have a model or the tools to help him grow specifically in his areas of need. There were moments when he felt the temptation to mimic his father's behaviors, but instead of giving in to them, he chose a different one. He learned how to be physically present while keeping his emotions at a distance, not better but different. He called that "playing ghost"! He'd be physically present, but his mind and emotions would be miles away, just like that O'Jays song goes, "Your Body's Here with Me (But Your Mind's on the Other Side of Town)." It's a place I know all too well – my father was the same way, being physically present but emotionally checked out. John didn't even realize he was emotionally escaping until his wife confronted him about it. In his mind, if he was physically there, everything should be cool, no harm, no foul. Ahh, WRONG! Things weren't all right. He might've been fine because he learned the ghost method early on, but his wife and kids didn't know the ghost method, and they didn't want to learn it, either. He'd seem fine until he was faced with triggering situations. That's when he becomes stoic, shut down, and unresponsive. Right there, that was his danger zone.

This coping mechanism may have protected him from repeating his father's abusive patterns, but it also created a barrier between him, his wife, and his children. By turning inward, John unintentionally made it difficult for his family to connect with him on an emotional level. John's narrative is one that resonates with many men today, as their desire to be free and vulnerable is often overshadowed by the fear of letting go and facing the unknown. This was an ongoing battle within John, a struggle between his desire to open up and his instinct to protect himself from rejection and pain. Sometimes, that struggle would leave him feeling alone, even when he was surrounded by friends and loved ones. It was a constant tug-of-war between the vulnerability that could lead to healing and the self-protection mechanisms that kept him emotionally imprisoned. John's story highlights the importance of providing support and guidance to young boys immediately as they navigate their emotional landscape. Creating a safe landing space will allow them to express their feelings and help them understand the complexities of their emotions, we can empower them to develop healthier coping strategies, give them tools to embrace and manage their feelings, and avoid the pitfalls of emotional disconnection as we guide the next generation of boys into manhood.

For John, his journey toward healing began when he started to confront his past and recognize its impact on his present relationships. Through therapy, support groups, and honest conversations with his family, John began dismantling the walls he had built around his emotions. As he learned to let go of fear and embrace vulnerability, he forged deeper connections with his loved ones, allowing them to know and understand him truly. Although his journey to healing was difficult, he knew it was worth taking. As he talked about the emotional distance he had created from his family, the pain in his eyes revealed how he felt. He wished to escape that pattern and demonstrate to them how much they really mattered to him, but his past was too much of a burden. It was heartbreaking to witness a man so committed to being a better father and husband yet struggle to overcome the barriers he had unknowingly placed around his own heart. John's self-made prison held him captive, leaving him waiting in vain for someone to come and save him or guide him out of the darkness that enveloped his heart. The feeling of helplessness was overwhelming, and the yearning for a guiding light grew stronger with each passing day.

In the presence of the men in that group, John found a heartfelt affirmation and love, creating an experience he had never known before. It was as though he was released from the chains of his "daddy wounds" amidst those men. John was determined that he wouldn't allow another day to pass without addressing the unresolved issues in his relationships. Despite his children being adults and having their own lives, he felt the urgency to heal any remaining wounds. He couldn't let the sands of time slip by without sharing his story, expressing his feelings, offering his apologies, growing with them, and taking steps towards a fresh start. Sadly, many shy away from such groups, perceiving them as signs of weakness or considering them odd.

Yet, I stand by the belief that participating in these gatherings is a display of strength and courage, and it provides a platform for accountability. The Bible attests, 'in the multitude of counsel, there is safety', and that's precisely what John found – safety within the multitude of that group. John's tears that day originated from a profoundly deep place within him. It was as if the little boy within him had been yearning for this his entire life, a sanctuary to call home.

This exchange really helped me unlock a whole new drive to help men become UNbroken. Just like John, countless boys and men are left to navigate life on their own, scraping together any resources they can find to make sense of it all. It's a struggle that's all too common and one that weighs heavily on their hearts. By creating safe spaces for men to share their experiences, emotions, and vulnerabilities, we can help them break free from the chains of their past and embrace a future filled with healing, growth, and genuine connection. In doing so, we can work together to break the cycle of brokenness and foster a new generation of whole, emotionally healthy intelligent men who can lead and love with strength and compassion.

When we look at grown, strong, burly men, it's easy to forget that they, too, were once little boys. Innocent, vulnerable little boys who longed for their father's touch and needed guidance. But, for some, that touch never came; that guidance never arrived. Instead, they were left feeling abandoned and forgotten, with the pain of neglect still lingering deep within their souls. As these little boys become men, they carry those unaddressed wounds with them, often struggling to break free from the chains of their past. We need to bear in mind the hearts of these men, for within them may still reside the boys they once were.

The love and support they need on their journey towards healing and growth could be unfulfilled, tucked away within. It's astonishing to think that despite the outward success, be it families, cars, homes, substantial wealth, esteemed professions such as doctors, lawyers, police officers, musicians, influencers, CEOs of Fortune 500 companies, or even preachers - within them might still be that little boy. That little boy who's still nursing his wounds, drenched in fear, feeling forsaken, or grappling to decipher life's puzzles on his own. I've seen firsthand how young boys, left to navigate the challenges of manhood alone, can end up lost and misguided men. We must recognize the vulnerability and social influences these boys face today and find ways to guide and support them as they walk the path to manhood (social media, exposure to lewd acts via the internet, television; etc.).

JUNK DRAW

During my journey, I found myself not only identifying with John but also with a set of screws. My wife and I received a used IKEA bed for our son, Levi, as a gift from our cousins Eric and Lasonya. The bed was perfect – a loft style with a spacious area underneath, providing Levi with a place to play. When we inspected the bed, I knew it was just what Levi needed. I expressed my gratitude to Eric and Lasonya and informed them that I'd return to collect the bed the following week. However, I was soon reminded of the notorious complexity of IKEA's assembly instructions, especially for a used bed. When I asked if they had the instructions, they regretfully admitted and chuckled at the same time that they didn't have the instructions. Eric hysterically belted out, "Good luck"! At that moment, I knew it was going to be a problem, but I shrugged it off and told myself, "Shon, you got this don't trip, you'll figure it out!" Filled with mixed emotions and wondering if I should really tackle this project, I decided to do so. Just like a new father running into fatherhood without a roadmap or instructions I hesitantly pursued it.

I brought the bed back to Flint from Detroit the following week and got started. As I started putting the bed together, I carefully arranged the bed parts all around the room. My master plan was coming together; until it wasn't. Deep down inside, I was hoping this project would be more like putting together a five-piece puzzle, rather than a five-thousand-piece puzzle. I was dead set on finding a way to piece it all together without getting lost in the weeds of screws and bolts. Somewhere during the process, my wife offered to search the internet for assembly instructions, I declined and assured her that I had everything under control. Knowing full well that I didn't have it all together, that was just my good ol' pride and ego talking. Look, I made up my mind that I was here now and there was no way I was going back. I wanted the bed, I asked for the bed, and I had to figure it out on my own. "I don't need instructions; I'm gonna show her that her husband and Levi's dad got this." Y'all, I knew I was setting myself up for failure. I should have let her go to IKEA's website and find the instructions, but my ego wouldn't let me.

I convinced myself that the owner's manual would be hard to find, and besides, those instructions can be so freaking confusing to read anyway. Just like me trying to put this bed together without any instructions. Many men journey along similar paths as they step into manhood. They often find themselves battling with life's challenges without a map or guide. I was trying to assemble that bed without a single clue.

Faced with the tasks of becoming fathers, sons, and husbands, we wrestle with piecing together our roles and responsibilities from bits and pieces of our own experiences or the few examples we've seen around us. In doing so, we force ourselves to fit into society's expectations, even when it doesn't feel right or goes against who we truly are on the inside. Going with the flow can lead to a sense of accomplishment on the surface, but underneath lies the potential for instability and uncertainty. Just as a poorly assembled bed wobbles or comes apart, a man's life built without proper guidance can lead to unresolved issues and a shaky foundation, affecting not only himself but also his family and loved ones. It's crucial to recognize this challenge and the need for clearer roadmaps to guide men on their journey into manhood, so they can build solid lives, relationships, and families without leaving loose screws behind.

After hours of assembly, I felt incredibly accomplished when I finally put the bed together. I admired my work, thinking, "I did this all by myself!" I took a close look at my handiwork, and something seemed a little off. And it was, I noticed three extra screws on the floor with no apparent home. A few minutes later, my wife called out to ask if I was done, I quickly hid the screws in my pocket and invited her to see the finished product. She declined to try it out herself and was very wary of its stability to hold adult weight. I told Levi to give it a go. As he climbed up, she noticed the bed was a little wobbly and asked if anything was missing or off. I assured her that the bed was cool, and I'll figure it out. Trying to deflect her attention from obvious shortcomings, I urged her to appreciate the positive outcomes instead of highlighting the negatives in my work.

I'll admit, I was aware of something wrong when I discovered the three extra screws. Yet, I wasn't ready to take responsibility. I couldn't muster the courage to tell my wife that I was clueless about the placement of those spare screws. So, I chose to stash them away in the garage's junk drawer - a final destination for all my remaining bits and pieces from numerous projects. Similarly, some men might relegate their emotional immaturity and inadequacies to the "junk drawers" of life, an evasion tactic to escape accountability and confront the evident issues at hand, even if only obvious to themselves. Their dodging and reluctance to address their childhood traumas and life decisions can have a profound effect on their children. My father, for instance, either sidestepped dealing with his personal trauma or was oblivious to its existence.

This brings me to a recent event at InvolvedDad, where we had an intern join us for a semester. She was working on a project to devise a tool to spot fathers within our program who either had limited engagement with their children or found it challenging to be active and engaged dads. Her research investigated if the father's parenting methods were shaped by their own bonds with their fathers. What the results uncovered was that a significant number of these fathers held an atypical outlook on their own parenting, as well as their parents. They often placed their mothers on pedestals as saints of perfection while demonizing their absent fathers. Oddly enough, they subjected the mothers of their children to the same exact standards they held their own fathers to, criticizing them while singing their own praises, even in the face of their own paternal shortcomings. They failed to draw a parallel between the repeating patterns of their fathers' behaviors and their own. Even though they found numerous reasons to account for their own absence, they offered little understanding for their fathers who were either absent or not actively involved. This mindset seemed to be an offshoot of watching their mothers grapple with difficulties. They sided with their mothers over their fathers, even though their actions mirrored those of their fathers.

Instead of examining their own roles in the situation, these men identified as victims, identifying with their own mothers as if their circumstances were one and the same. This revelation underscores the importance of addressing the lack of guidance and supports many boys experience as they transition into manhood, husbandhood, and fatherhood. The cycle of brokenness perpetuates itself when boys grow up without the guidance and support needed to navigate their journey into manhood. By breaking this cycle, we can foster healthier parental relationships and empower future generations to thrive.

HITTING THE RESET

Reflecting on the scenario with the bed construction and my reluctance to admit my error to my wife, I fell back on an all-too-familiar response - I avoided and masked up. This wasn't an isolated instance; I had resorted to this tactic when I was 10, at 17, and even at 35. Doesn't that echo Adam's behavior in the Garden of Eden? After disobeying God, Adam chose to hide. In the end, he mended his bond with his father through sacrifice, and that's the path I needed to tread. But until that point, my instinct was to flee.

At the age of 10, I found myself habitually reaching for the reset button, and not just metaphorically. While immersed in video games with my buddy Remy, I would hit the reset button at the first sign of defeat. Too inexperienced to grasp the implications of my actions, I was unwittingly conditioning myself to bail out at the first sign of trouble. This tendency stuck with me as I grew, making me prone to throwing in the towel or seeking a 'reset' when things got tough. Now, there's no harm in hitting reset per se. The issue arises when the reset becomes an excuse to quit, rather than an opportunity to reassess and make better choices.

This habitual avoidance of challenges reared its head once again when I was 17. I had the privilege of playing football at Michigan State University, but I hit that all-too-familiar reset button yet again. With the firing of my then-coach, George Perles, and the introduction of Nick Saban - now steering the Alabama Crimson Tide - the game changed. Saban brought with him a set of expectations and a disciplined approach that was foreign to me. He was intent on fostering a winning culture, one driven by discipline and meticulous process – virtues I hadn't yet adopted consistently. Faced with this challenge, I recoiled. I fell back into the trap of making excuses and ultimately quit, turning my back not just on my team and myself, but also on the prospect of a potential NFL career.

Saban could never have understood the complexities of my past - I was barely beginning to comprehend them myself. The pain of my father's rejection, telling me I was too small for college football, had etched a deep and enduring scar on my psyche. Consequently, when Saban challenged me, I fought back with unexpected fierceness. It was like facing another rejection, and I instinctively defended myself, shadowboxing an invisible enemy from my past. My unresolved childhood trauma, which had quietly nested within me, had now become my constant companion, silently influencing my decisions, and coloring my perception of opportunities for personal growth.

My father's rejection had created within me an ingrained distrust of men, distorting my judgment and decision-making processes. More often than not, we act impulsively, without a clear understanding of the driving force behind our decisions. My past interactions with my father cast a long shadow on my attempts to build and maintain trustful relationships. Eventually, I began the critical journey of internal healing and self-discovery, a journey that holds the power to truly transform our lives.

During my marital strife, I could trace the origins of my troubles back to the emotional trauma inflicted by my father's dismissive words. Despite my earnest attempts at being a loving husband to my wife, I found myself sabotaging our relationship, driven by a compulsive need to disprove my father's assertion that I was 'too small.' My wife had never considered me inadequate or incapable of leading our family, yet my insecurities would often convince me otherwise. I had allowed the ghost of my father's judgment to creep into my marriage, prompting me to measure my worth by how much respect and admiration I felt I was receiving from my wife.

And so, even at 35, I lost sight of my priorities, allowing my unresolved issues to divert my attention away from the most important aspects of my life - my family. My self-sabotaging behaviors unknowingly undermined the strong foundation my wife and I were trying to establish. My obsession with proving my worth and avoiding any feeling of insignificance began to strain our marriage, putting at risk the most valuable thing in my life. Much like those hidden screws in the garage, I had stashed away my insecurities, allowing them to subtly sabotage my relationships and opportunities, until I finally confronted them, initiating my journey of healing and self-discovery.

Reflecting upon these three decisive stages in my life - at the ages of 10, 17, and 35 - I noticed an unsettling pattern of surrendering to adversity and giving up prematurely. This is a path, I realized, that is all too familiar to many men in their journey toward manhood. The vulnerable inner child that resides within us often lacks the necessary wisdom and tools needed for healing and 'Growing-Through.'

'Growing-Through' refers to the process of consciously navigating and embracing life's most difficult challenges. Instead of shying away from these tough situations, we face them head-on, acknowledging their potential to shape us into the individuals we were destined to be, enabling us to unlock our fullest potential.

In connection with my previous reflection, it's crucial to recognize that this process of 'Growing-Through' requires us to confront our past traumas and insecurities, much like I had to face my father's hurtful remarks and the impact they had on my life. Just as I unearthed those hidden screws that were subtly sabotaging my relationships, we must dig deep to uncover and heal from our past wounds to truly progress and thrive in our lives.

When a man struggles with releasing his inner child from past traumas or unfulfilled needs, it becomes exceedingly challenging for him to guide his own children through similar trials and embark on their path to healing. Instead of charting new courses, these men often resort to their personal experiences, directing their children to "do as I say, not as I do." Kids, however, can spot the inconsistency between words and actions. They are shaped more profoundly by what we do than what we say.

While children might temporarily conform to the behaviors we prescribe, without consistent demonstrations of the right choices and emotional regulation, these shifts tend not to endure. The practical, hands-on example of a father living out his words often goes unseen. What we have are broken men who were once broken boys. Numerous men are navigating life burdened with unresolved traumas, yet they find it less frightening to neglect the work of self-improvement and instead parent from the wounded spaces of their past.

Had I been honest with my wife about the shaky condition of the bed and its need for repair, she may have been initially stumped about where to begin, but she would have plunged right into the problem and sought a solution - a quality many women exhibit when confronted with the absence of a father figure. While my wife could have certainly taken on the task of rectifying the bed, it would have been more daunting as it wasn't her traditional role in our home. Countless women are raising boys, and they're doing a phenomenal job. However, it's important to note that women, by nature, aren't designed to shoulder the primary responsibility of grooming a boy into a man. This doesn't reduce their capabilities or contributions, but it highlights the significance of shared roles in parenting. My wife and I synergize remarkably in raising our kids. We agreed that she'd spearhead guiding Shelby and Sydni when it came to matters about girls and thank God for that! Trust me, the complexities that arise with them sometimes make me want to throw up a peace sign and say, "I'm out!" But, of course, I don't. I interject when necessary, providing a male perspective on their situations.

In many households, boys learn from an early age that crying is not acceptable from both moms and dads. They are confronted with phrases like, "If you cry, I'll give you something to cry about." Afraid of the repercussions of expressing their feelings, these boys remain silent and form their own conclusions, which only serve to amplify their emotional pain and perpetuate their suffering. Looking back on my own history, I can't help but wish I had been more open about my emotions with my mother and had the chance to do the same with my father. This openness could have given them the chance to guide me through the tumultuous emotional journey I was on. They could have helped me make sense of the whirlwind of feelings that were, at times, so overwhelming. By keeping my emotions locked away, I denied them - and myself - the opportunity to understand and address the pain I was carrying. It's a lesson I've carried into my own parenting and something I hope more fathers will understand: our feelings are not our enemy and sharing them with those we trust is a strength, not a weakness.

Like those screws I placed in the drawer, I felt like an extra part from a do-it-yourself project – unused, misplaced, and left behind. It took time for me to realize that my self-worth wasn't tied to my father's recognition or approval. By asking tough questions and seeking answers, I discovered my value beyond the confines of my father's relationship with me. If you're in a similar predicament, don't be afraid to search for answers and express your emotions. This can offer much-needed context and understanding, helping you to heal and grow. Always remember, just like those overlooked screws, you possess purpose and value, even if it's not immediately evident to those around you.

The process of assembling that wobbly bed becomes a striking metaphor for many young men navigating the uncertain path to manhood. They often find themselves with imperfect instructions, attempting to piece together their identity with tools that might not fit the task. The charismatic personality down the street, the well-meaning but misguided uncle, or perhaps the absent father—these are the imperfect templates they have to shape their masculinity. While I will spotlight many incredible fathers and father figures in the upcoming chapters, it's important to confront the reality that the scars of early life traumas can cast long shadows on a man's life, a fact that resonates through a wealth of data.

Young men, in their search for identity, often look up to musicians, athletes, or social media influencers. But what do they see when they switch on the TV? They're bombarded with exaggerated and often harmful portrayals of masculinity. Their peers, who should ideally provide support, are often as lost as they are, navigating the same murky waters of manhood. Even more worryingly, they may encounter destructive notions of masculinity within their own homes. It's a sobering reality we must face if we aim to guide young men toward a healthier, more positive expression of their masculinity. The streets can often serve as the unwilling teachers of manhood, particularly in urban neighborhoods grappling with crime and poverty. Here, the lessons imparted are often about aggression, violence, and substance abuse. The media, too, plays a critical role, painting a distorted, toxic picture of masculinity that glorifies aggression, dominance, and emotional repression. Peers can also exert a powerful influence, pushing young men to conform to risky behaviors or attitudes, particularly when they lack the guidance of positive male role models.

Growing up, my neighborhood was a sea of women and children, with few men in sight. The older guys on the block, who were barely out of their teens, assumed the mantle of manhood in our eyes. We admired them for their cars, their money, and the attention they received from girls. Yet, many of them were thrust into these roles prematurely due to the absence of their fathers. This was during the early days of the crack-cocaine epidemic, which drew many young men into the vortex of addiction or crime. These painful memories are a constant reminder of the importance of my work at InvolvedDad, where we strive to help fathers become more present and engaged in their children's lives, thereby fostering stronger men, families, and communities. Yet, it is crucial to remember that we can overcome these restrictive notions of masculinity. The key lies in seeking out positive male role models, challenging toxic messages about masculinity, and creating space for alternate expressions of manhood.

The critical question to ponder upon is - how does a boy become a man if he has never seen one? This brings us to a harsh reality. Unaddressed trauma in a boy's life can lead to a broken man, one who struggles to make sound decisions as a father, a husband, and a leader. This cycle can be broken, but it requires us to redefine masculinity in healthier, more inclusive terms. Every individual has the right to define their version of masculinity. By doing so, we can aspire to a society that values and respects all individuals, regardless of their gender identity or expression, and enables boys to grow into emotionally healthy, balanced men.

-2-
WORDS THAT DESTTROY

As a young boy, I was hungry for attention, parched, and yearning for an emotional connection that seemed to flow so freely between my father and my older brother, Travis. This connection, this bond, was something that I craved, something I would have done anything to gain. The craving for my father's approval, his validation, and his attention was a constant undercurrent in my life. It was an elusive currency, always just beyond my reach, the pursuit of which colored my every decision and action.

Travis and my father had a relationship that was bathed in the warm light of friendship and shared interests. Travis was a sportsman, a pretty good athlete in his high school days. I can still remember them standing on the sidelines, talking, laughing, sharing a world that seemed so alien to me. My father wasn't an affectionate man, but with Travis, he was engaging, invested, and present. My older sister, Saria, held a different charm in my father's life. I thought she was his favorite. It wasn't her doing; it was my father's evident preference that painted her in these colors of favoritism. Saria never made me, or my other siblings

34

feel lesser, but the specter of favoritism loomed, casting long shadows on my relationship with my father. Then, there was me. As a sophomore transitioning into my junior year, I began to make a name for myself in the world of football. I thought this was it, my golden ticket to my father's world, the key to unlocking the bond I envied between him and Travis. The whispers of my talent began to grow louder in my city and amongst national football powerhouses, and with them, my hope was to draw my father's attention. One day, a letter from the University of Notre Dame arrived. I was extremely excited and decided I was going to wait on the porch and share the news with my father when he arrived. Notre Dame was his favorite team at the time. That letter, a sign of my budding talent, held the promise of the connection I yearned for. I imagined his face lighting up with pride once I showed him the letter. Hopefully shared laughter and engaging conversations would begin. I clung to the hope and that letter as if it was a lifeline, my heart throbbing with anticipation as I decided to share the news. I sat on the porch that day, the letter clutched tightly in my hand, waiting for him to arrive. As his old-school Cadillac turned the corner and approached our house, my heart pounded in my chest, each beat echoing with excitement and anxiety. As he parked and stepped out, time seemed to slow down, each step he took toward me echoing like a drumbeat in the silence. "Nate, look," I said, my voice trembling slightly. I've always called him Nate, a practice rooted in a complex history that didn't make it any less painful. I wanted to call him 'Dad', but that privilege was kept from me, a story for another time. He glanced at the letter several times, and then at me. We locked eyes, and at that moment, I dared to hope. I dared to believe that this was our moment of connection, our breakthrough. But then, he spoke the words that shattered my heart and my hope into a million pieces.

"You're too small," he said, the words hanging in the air like a death sentence. He handed me back the letter, his face void of any emotion, and walked away. At that moment, my heart crumbled. I was devastated, hurt, and angry.

Anger became a shield, protecting my broken heart from further disappointment. A callousness began to form around my heart, tough and unyielding. I found myself trapped in a whirlwind of resentment and discontent, against my father, against any man who dared to tell me what I could or could not do.

My journey into manhood began that day, on the porch, with a letter from the University of Notre Dame and three heartbreaking words: "You're too small." Little did I know then how much these words would shape me, and how they would become a catalyst for change. We've all had those moments, haven't we? Moments where our hearts were trampled upon, our dreams dismissed, our hopes crushed under the weight of someone else's words. Perhaps you can relate to my story. Maybe you too have been told that you were "too small," not in size, but in potential, capability, and in worth.

Remember that teacher who scoffed at your dreams, telling you that you were not smart enough to achieve them? Or that time when your mother, in a fit of anger or disappointment, declared that you would end up just like your absent or flawed father, embedding in you a seed of doubt about your future? Remember the sharp sting of embarrassment when you were teased for your worn-out clothes, the hole in your shoe, or the outdated phone you carried? The social media attacks, those moments when your financial circumstance became a punchline for others, marking you as 'less than' in their eyes. Or perhaps you were the guy all the cool girls laughed at and called you ugly and refused to go to the 8th-grade dance or the prom with you. Silently enduring the cruel taunts about your appearance, each joke taking a blow to your self-esteem. Maybe you know the pain of being the 'other', the one who doesn't fit in, the one who is always on the outside looking in. The one who had to navigate a maze of cultural entanglements, just to fit in.

We all have our version of 'too small'. We all bear scars from past wounds, echoes of unkind words that we've internalized and carried with us into adulthood. These experiences, though painful, are not unique to me or you. They are universal threads in the fabric of human experience. The key lies not in the hurtful words themselves, but in how we choose to respond. We can let these words define us, keep us small, keep us shackled, or we can choose to rise above them, to grow bigger, stronger, and more resilient.

THE WEIGHT OF WORDS

The weight of my father's words, the statement that I was "too small," seemed to loom larger than life itself. Unbeknownst to him, I was already battling a silent war with my own self-confidence and self-worth. His dismissive comment did nothing but validate the insecurities I had been combatting, and it felt as if I had lost yet another round in the ring of life.

Despite my athleticism and my intellect, I found myself repeatedly on the losing side of battles. Whether it was pursuing a girl who did not feel the same way I felt about her, losing at video games, or feeling whack because of the clothes I wore, the sting of defeat was a constant companion. These were private battles that no one knew about, the internal struggles of a young boy who was yet to learn how to articulate his feelings, even to his own mother. I recall those times when I would ask my mom, returning from rejection, "Am I cute?" She would always, always answer, "Yes, you are cute. You are very handsome." However, her words did little to satisfy my insecurities. I would respond, "You're just saying that because you're my mother. You're supposed to say that." My mother's attempts at validating me felt hollow, not because she didn't mean them, but because the one person whose approval I craved the most remained elusive. My father's apparent acceptance of others, compared with his perceived rejection of me, was a wound that cut deep. I know now that that wasn't his intended purpose to inflict such emotional distress, but his actions, or lack thereof, left a lasting imprint on my psyche. The sound of his rejection echoed louder than my mother's acceptance, and his silence spoke volumes.

The pressure of this constant quest for validation was a crippling insecurity that vividly colored every aspect of my life. This situation intensified when my neighborhood fell prey to the crack cocaine epidemic. Boys with whom I used to play sports or hang out, began to drift away, lured by the magnetism of the drug game. Suddenly, popularity wasn't about who was the best athlete or the funniest guy in class, it was about who had the most money, who was part of the 'in' crowd. Boys who were once insignificant or corny became the center of attention, thanks to the drug game and the big homies. This shift in social dynamics only served to amplify my feelings of inadequacy and rejection. Despite my insecurities, I became skilled at hiding them behind the facade of athleticism, wit, and politeness. To the outside world, I was doing just fine. But on the inside, I was anything but. The battle with my insecurities was a lonely one, fought in the silent corners of my heart.

UNMASKING JEALOUSY - THE HIDDEN BATTLE

Several years after my daughter Sydni's birth, I found myself in a moment of profound vulnerability. I was about to confess to my wife an unspoken battle I had been fighting internally for years. I had an unwelcomed guest living within me, an unwanted tenant who had taken up residence within. This intrusive guest was feeding off my insecurities, growing stronger with every moment of discontent. It was jealousy, but not a random one. It was specifically aimed at those who mirrored my own image, black men. I remember the fear and concern I possessed as I started to share this with my wife, "Promise me you'll hear me out before you judge," I pleaded. The terror of judgment was real, how would my wife look at me? The self-confident, secure, inspirational man she married had chinks in his armor. He was really flawed, broken, and in need of internal healing. He was an imposter! But I was ready to expose this festering wound. My jealousy was towards successful black men, men who were my colleagues, and men whom I perceived to be doing better than me. If they were doing better than me, the gnawing feeling of jealousy would consume me from the inside out. I would tell myself stories to cope with it. I'd convince myself they were only doing well in life because they were involved in illegal activity, they didn't earn what they had, or some other bogus justifiable ignorant thought I evoked in my head. Just saying this aloud makes me sad and angry at the same time. However, I knew it wasn't right and that wasn't God's best for me. I made a commitment to help others grow from my mistakes, even if it was at my own expense of exposing myself and becoming more vulnerable.

My conclusion about those black men was a lie, a far cry from the truth, but it was the only way I could justify my feelings at the time. Living with such jealousy was like being chained to a relentless beast. It gnawed at me continuously. I was cheering on the outside, but secretly wrestling on the inside. This emotion, born out of rejection and fueled by the trials of my youth, had remained hidden until I chose to confront it. My jealousy was masked behind everything else, any and everything I could mask it with, sex, pornography, sports, looking cool, name-dropping, and even giving off the aura of false humility.

But now, the stakes were higher, much higher. I didn't want my daughter to inherit this toxic emotion or trait, this gnawing jealousy that I'd been battling. There's a verse in the Bible that speaks about the fathers eating sour grapes and setting their children's teeth on edge. I didn't want my own sour grapes of jealousy and insecurity to cause my daughter any distress in her life. I didn't want her to suffer from my wrong thinking. It wasn't fair to my wife or our children to have to deal with unresolved issues of mine. I was ready to face it head-on. I shared with my wife privately and then my church community the struggle I had been dealing with my whole life. It wasn't about seeking sympathy or collective support. It was about personal accountability. It was about the commitment to breaking this cycle of jealousy, to ensure it didn't pass on to my precious daughter or generations to come.

CONFRONTING OUR INTERNAL DEMONS - FOR OURSELVES AND OUR FUTURE

I understand that it may be extremely difficult for you to confront, let alone disclose, your internal struggles. These are your hidden secrets, your silent battles that hold you captive in their unrelenting grip. We often believe that as long as these issues remain hidden, as long as nobody else is aware of them, we can manage. "I'm fine," we reassure ourselves, but this is far from the truth.

Our past experiences and our history profoundly shape how we process information, make decisions, and draw conclusions. One of my close friends, George Conway, who also happens to be a therapist, often compares our brains to a computer when discussing trauma. When you surf the Internet and begin to type a word into the search bar, a drop-down menu will appear, suggesting searches based on your history. Our brains work in a similar manner. We might pretend that the trauma of our past doesn't exist, if as long as we don't discuss it, we don't have to deal with it. Yet, all it takes is a single trigger for that 'drop-down menu' in our brain to appear, for us to react from a place of past hurt and trauma. Our brains are like a computer, storing and remembering past searches, and past experiences. I could have pretended that my jealousy was a thing of the past, that I had moved on, and all was well. However, confronting it was crucial for my growth and healing. Understand, I'm not suggesting that you should disclose your personal struggles to others. That's a decision that's entirely up to you. However, I am urging you to confront the demons that you've kept hidden, the ones you've refused to acknowledge. Perhaps it's the echoing voice of being 'too small' that you've carried around. Allow me to tell you this - you are not too small. You are big enough, strong enough, intelligent enough, and capable enough. You possess the resilience to overcome any obstacle or challenge that your past throws at you.

Remember, confronting these internal struggles is not just about finding peace for ourselves, but also about ensuring that we don't pass on our unresolved issues to our children. It's about breaking the cycle, making sure that our 'sour grapes' don't set our children's teeth on edge. We owe it to ourselves and our children to confront our past, to heal, and to grow beyond it. This journey may be difficult, but rest assured, it's one worth taking.

REVISITING OUR TRAUMA - A PERSONAL ENCOUNTER

In the not-too-distant past, an incident occurred that demonstrated to me, in a painfully personal way, how deeply our past traumas can continue to affect us. My daughter, Shelby, faced a dilemma at school with a group of girls. Those who know Shelby would tell you she's the type of girl who avoids conflict whenever possible. Unlike her older sister Sydni, who doesn't mind a good altercation if it presented itself. Sydni is the child who shares every aspect of her life with us, sometimes to her detriment, whereas Shelby is more reserved. She's introverted, not fond of being the center of attention, and dislikes the idea of causing anyone disappointment or anger. We sensed something was wrong at school when Shelby began acting differently. We discovered a group of girls was targeting her, looking to provoke a fight. Her mother and I advised her differently: her mother preached avoidance, de-escalation, and conflict resolution; whereas I leaned towards preparation for a physical confrontation if the situation didn't improve. This situation persisted for weeks. My advice was increasingly moving towards the necessity of a physical altercation as a resolution, much to my wife's disapproval. Then, one day, we received a call from the school. Shelby was to be suspended. She had been involved in a near fight. We were defensive, knowing the girls had been harassing Shelby, and we also knew Shelby didn't want to fight. We adamantly pressed the school to conduct a more thorough investigation before drawing any conclusions. The ensuing investigation unveiled that Shelby, though not physically involved in a fight, was one of the instigators. She had rallied a friend to assist her in intimidating these girls, which the school labels as a near-fight incident, which is grounds for suspension. I vented my anger and frustration to a friend whose daughter was also tangled in this mess. As my ranting escalated, and persisted he posed a question that caught me off guard, "Is this really about Shelby, or is it about something else?" I believed it was about Shelby until he asked that question. He probed further, questioning if I had a history of being bullied as a child. That's when an old, unresolved incident from when I was 13 came flooding back. This situation with my daughter was echoing that unresolved trauma, much like a keyword search on your computer or laptop. Triggering a flow of related memories and emotions.

That evening, as I drove Shelby home from soccer practice, I cautiously raised the subject of the altercation. I inquired about what she was feeling, and what thoughts were racing through her mind during the incident. As expected, Shelby, a crier by nature and innately reluctant to cause harm to others, burst into tears. She cried not just a few, but a river of tears. I was inclined to join her in her tears, believing that her suspension and the girls' harassment were the sources of her distress. However, when I delved deeper, asking her why she was crying, her response left me breathless: "I didn't want to fight Daddy, I was afraid, and you kept telling me to fight and that's not what I wanted to do!" A wave of remorse came over me. I had been the one encouraging her to fight, to confront this situation head-on, when it was completely opposed to her nature. At that moment, it dawned on me: I was parenting from a place of my own unresolved trauma.

At the age of 13, I was threatened by a boy at school. He had told everyone that he was going to beat me up after school, and the news spread like wildfire. Consumed by fear, I spent the entire day in dread and slept in every class because of the looming showdown. When the time came, my cousin Alicia, renowned for her courage and fighting capabilities, stepped in on my behalf. She dared the boy to fight her first if he wanted to fight me. The fight was prevented, but the incident seared itself into my memory. Now, as I saw my daughter in a similar situation, I realized I was attempting to rectify my past through her. I was still grappling with the ghost of my 13-year-old self, the boy who avoided the fight, who was overwhelmed by fear. That boy, whom I had unjustly labeled a coward, weak, and soft, had taken root in me, and I was unconsciously projecting this onto Shelby. I was trapped in the belief that she had to meet her troubles head-on, just as I wished I had done all those years ago. My own trauma was dictating my advice to her, not what she truly needed or wanted. She didn't need to fight. My duty was to steer her through this situation with understanding and empathy, something I had desired from my own father. But I failed in that pivotal moment. After Shelby's heartfelt admission, I apologized profusely. Our tears blended as I confessed that I had been unknowingly overlaying my trauma onto her, pushing her into a battle she had neither the desire nor the necessity to fight. That night, in prayer, I sought God's guidance. His wisdom urged me to extend grace and mercy to that frightened 13-year-old boy within me, to cease imposing negative connotations and judging him, and free him from his distant past.

I extend this part of my journey to you, not as a badge of shame, but as a beacon of hope. I want you to know that it's possible to break free from the chains of our past and the voices that tell you that "you're 'too small'. By confronting and dealing with these voices, you can start to let go of their hold on you. you can free yourselves from the chains they've put on you. So, I challenge you, just like I did myself, to confront your demons. To shed light on your hidden struggles. To take steps towards healing. Because by acknowledging and addressing these issues, we can start to move past them. We can start to grow from being "too small' to becoming "big enough".

-3-

THE MASK WE WEAR

Men may not embellish their faces with layers of eyeshadow or apply the gloss of lipstick to their lips, but do not be misled; we too are versed in the art of disguise. We too wrap ourselves in an array of masks, but they are not of latex or finely powdered cosmetics. Rather, they are formed from the rigid societal expectations, the gnawing anxieties birthed from personal insecurities, and the demanding pressure to embody the stereotypical portrayals of manhood.

Unlike theatrical masks, these aren't nestled on the topography of our faces. Instead, they are overlaid onto our very selves, engulfing our true identities so seamlessly that we often lose track of where the mask ceases and we begin. These are the masks of masculinity that, rather than projecting our individuality, echo the roles and behaviors that society has long considered apt for men.

The masks we will explore are as varied as they are abundant. The Lion, the Hyena, the Turtle, the Dog, the Chameleon, the Owl, and the Panda – each symbolizes a unique facet of the intricate prism of manhood, each offering a different strategy with which men traverse the stormy waters of societal expectations and personal insecurities.

While these masks may seem like protective armors, providing a hardened shell to retreat into or a ferocious facade to project, underneath them often lies a man grappling with his vulnerabilities, fears, and a yearning to express his authentic self without judgment or mockery. Beneath the roaring pride of the Lion, the adaptive laughter of the Hyena, or the quiet shelter of the Turtle, resides a man yearning for connection, understanding, and the acceptance of his true self.

The Lion mask is the guise of the man who conceals himself behind his pride and possessions. The Hyena mask is the garb of the one who transforms himself into a character unrecognizable, just to blend in with the crowd. The Turtle mask is the shell of the man who isolates himself from the world, battling his internal demons in solitude. Each mask reflects a different facet of the distorted image of manhood we often feel obliged to portray. Like the makeup women wear, these masks cast an illusion of confidence, strength, and invincibility, enabling us to hide our vulnerabilities, fears, and insecurities. But simultaneously, they obscure our authentic selves. As I reassured my wife that she didn't need makeup to define her beauty, it is vital for us, as men, to understand that we don't need these masks to earn value or respect.

In this chapter, we'll venture deep into the exploration of these masculine masks, scrutinizing their origins, implications, and impacts on men and their relationships. Our goal is to unpack and understand these masks, fostering a future where every man feels empowered to express his authentic self without fear, judgment, and the compulsion to wear a mask. The seed of an idea sown early in boys is that vulnerability equates to weakness. Crying, a natural expression of emotion, is quickly labeled as a sign of weakness, likened to being 'soft' or 'like a girl' – a sentiment that must be hidden at all costs. This notion is perpetuated by influential figures in a child's life - older brothers, uncles, fathers, and even mothers, who constantly reinforce this idea, encouraging young boys to swallow their tears, don the Lion mask, and project an illusion of invincibility.

IMPRISONED IN PRISON

This paradigm is prevalent in spaces where perceived strength and toughness are paramount, such as in prisons. My experience as a prison chaplain confirmed this, as I saw men from diverse backgrounds and with various crimes on their records, all united by their embracing of the Lion mask. Whether incarcerated for heinous or petty crimes, many wore their masks as a necessary survival strategy in an environment that could exploit any sign of weakness. Behind the closed doors of my office, in the sanctuary of our one-on-one conversations, these men often felt secure enough to shed their masks. My wife has playfully dubbed me the "Man Whisperer," a testament to my uncanny ability to encourage men to bare their souls. I have found that men, who might otherwise bottle up their deepest emotions, feel compelled to share their innermost personal struggles almost immediately in my presence. I attribute this not to any special technique or strategy on my part, but rather to a divine gift bestowed upon me by my heavenly father.

When these men peel off their masks, they release an outpouring of raw emotion, revealing the deep-seated hurt, anger, trauma, and despair they've been harboring. Some of the most intimidating inmates, men who commanded respect and instilled fear within the prison community, would break down in my office. The sight of these hardened men thought to be resistant to emotion, weeping openly in my presence was a touching testament to the emotional turmoil they struggled with daily, yet felt compelled to hide it from the world. This glimpse into their private battles highlighted the absurdity between their true emotional state and the hardened exterior they felt forced to project. It revealed the oppressive burden of the Lion mask and the toll it takes on the mental health of men, who feel compelled to maintain a facade of immunity even as they grappled with intense emotional pain. The lion might be the king of the jungle, but even kings bear burdens. And just as the king's crown can weigh heavy on his head, so too can the Lion mask weigh heavy on the hearts of the men who wear it.

One inmate, a leader within the prison who projected an intimidating exterior, was a striking example of this. Known for his size and strength, and feared for his reputation, he commanded the respect of hundreds within the prison. Yet, in the solitude of my office, he disclosed his contemplations of self-harm and his profound sense of fear and openness, emotions he dared not show elsewhere. His story is not unique, however, it is a stark reminder of the pressures men face to uphold the Lion mask, to suppress their true emotions for fear of being seen as weak. This tendency is not confined to prison walls but extends to the free world. Many men, whether they are husbands, CEOs, or hold significant positions in society, wrestle with the same issues. They feel compelled to maintain a strong exterior, hide their vulnerabilities and fears, and uphold the Lion mask.

THE LION MASK

Many men adopt the Lion mask as a shield, seeking refuge behind an imposing facade of wealth and material possessions. Their goal is to project an image of success, power, and invisibility, often to compensate for feelings of insecurity and inadequacy. I, too, have worn the Lion mask. During the period when I struggled with jealousy, I used the lion mask to project a distorted image of myself. I borrowed the notoriety of my brother, who was a big-time street pharmacist in our community, using his position and influence to bolster mine. My athletic ability, served as a mask, providing me a passport into the circles of respect and acceptance. However, masks, by their nature, are fleeting. The spotlight that had once illuminated my athletic career began to dim when I could no longer play football. The roaring crowds, the praise, and the privileges I enjoyed faded away, and in their place came the sobering realization that I was no longer shielded by the Lion mask. Stripped of my notoriety and material possessions, I found myself standing alone, exposed, and vulnerable, contending with the unfamiliar environment of humility.

Many men also find themselves trapped in a ceaseless chase for wealth or "the bag," as it is informally termed. This pursuit, however, often diverts them from their true calling or "assignment." They accumulate fortunes, not out of a passion for their work or a genuine desire for material comfort, but as a means of reinforcing their persona of being all put together. This continual race for wealth, possessions, and trophies becomes their chosen path to project a specific image to the world. Caught in the grip of this illusion, these men believe that accruing wealth will bolster the image they wish to project to the world - an image of success, power, and invincibility. They are convinced that the grandeur of their possessions and the size of their bank accounts can sufficiently shield their insecurities and fears from the world. Unconsciously, their relentless pursuit of material wealth does not resolve their internal struggles; instead, it becomes a further extension of the Lion mask they wear.

However constant pursuit of wealth to uphold the Lion mask is a huge task. It is a chase with no finish line, driven by a skewed perception of self-worth that equates material wealth with personal value. It's a dangerous misconception that neglects the innate worth of an individual and their unique contributions to the world. Only by aligning our lives with our true purposes can we begin to dismantle the Lion mask and embrace our authentic selves, with all our vulnerabilities and strengths. This is the journey towards authentic manhood, a journey that requires us to cast aside societal expectations and summon the courage to stand in our truth, unshielded by the deceptive comfort of the Lion mask. They mistakenly believe that money can obscure their insecurities or indiscretions, not realizing that their flashy displays often serve to highlight their insecurities rather than conceal them. People who constantly broadcast their accomplishments or possessions are often trying to construct an image larger than life. Their goal is to assert dominance, to command respect, and to make others feel smaller in comparison. It's a misguided effort to elevate themselves by diminishing others, a strategy rooted in insecurity and self-doubt.

PUTTING IT TOGETHER

MANIFESTATIONS AND BEHAVIORS OF THE LION MASK:

1. **Pride and Arrogance**: Men wearing the Lion mask often display a high level of pride and arrogance, seemingly placing themselves above others. They tend to dominate conversations and often dismiss the opinions and feelings of others.

2. **Materialism:** They tend to measure their self-worth based on material success and possessions. They often flaunt their wealth, property, and luxury items as a testament to their perceived superiority.

3. **Aggression and Domination**: Men with the Lion mask might exhibit aggressive behavior, especially when their pride or authority is challenged. They may seek to dominate in all spheres, whether at work, in relationships, or in social situations, often resorting to intimidation or manipulation.

4. **Emotional Suppression:** These individuals tend to hide their vulnerabilities, fears, and insecurities. They might find it difficult to express emotions and show empathy, interpreting such behavior as signs of weakness.

PITFALLS OF THE LION MASK:

1. **Loneliness and Isolation**: The Lion mask can lead to isolation as it creates a barrier between the individual and others. People might feel intimidated or alienated due to the Lion's prideful and domineering behavior.

2. **Unresolved Emotional Issues**: The continual suppression of emotions can lead to unresolved emotional issues and mental health problems, such as depression, anxiety, and stress.

3. **Strained Relationships**: The Lion mask often negatively affects relationships. The lack of emotional openness and

empathy can strain relationships with family, friends, and partners.

4. **Lack of Self-Identity**: Men wearing the Lion mask often equate their self-worth with material possessions. When these are stripped away, they might struggle with self-identity and self-esteem.

REMOVING THE LION MASK:

1. **Self-Awareness:** The first step is to acknowledge and understand the Lion mask. Self-reflection and self-awareness exercises can help identify the instances when the mask is worn.

2. **Emotional Intelligence:** Developing emotional intelligence allows better management of emotions, encourages empathy, and fosters healthier relationships. It's about allowing oneself to feel, understand, and express emotions without fear of judgment or ridicule.

3. **Redefining Success and Self-worth**: It's important to redefine personal success and self-worth, not based on material possessions, but on personal growth, relationships, and contributions to society. This might involve identifying and pursuing one's "assignment" or unique purpose in life.

4. **Seek Professional Help:** Therapy or counseling can be beneficial in understanding and managing the issues related to the Lion Mask. A professional can provide tools and strategies to deal with suppressed emotions and build healthier self-perceptions.

Remember, removing the Lion Mask is a gradual process and requires patience and commitment. But, with persistence, it's possible to break free from the mask and embrace your authentic self-expression.

THE HYENA MASK:

Let's look at another type of mask, one I like to call the Hyena Mask. This is the mask worn by men who feel they need to blend in, to be part of the pack, often sidelining their true selves in the process. The guy under the Hyena Mask is a bit like a chameleon, shifting his vibe to match the crowd, laughing with everyone even when the joke doesn't land with him. His beliefs, his values, and even his personal dreams move around to fit the groupthink, and what he believes the world wants from him. He's convinced himself that this is the way, maybe even the best way, to get ahead or be accepted as one of the boys. But all this changing and adjusting stirs up a lot of inner conflicts.

The guy rocking the Hyena Mask buries his true self to earn approval. He's tiptoeing on thin ice, afraid of rejection, afraid of ridicule. He might be safe in the crowd, but he's giving up his unique voice in the process. This mask is worn by the men who get lost in the crowd. He tries to morph into something he's not, adjusting his moves to sync with the group's rhythm. He might even clown others, getting a cheap laugh at their expense. This dude becomes a social chameleon, blending in to give off that sense of belonging.

I have this childhood friend, a guy who was more on the introverted side, a guy that avoided conflict at every turn, and who respected everyone's unique qualities. That's what drew people towards him. He wasn't one to beef with others, but his quietness sometimes painted a target on him. People sometimes took his kindness for weakness. Instead of putting on the Lion Mask, trying to be all tough, and using his stuff to boost his image, he started rocking the Hyena Mask. He began joking at other guys' expense, especially when he was with certain groups. It was a whole 180 from who he was, the dude I knew - the guy who would keep his cool and stand up for others was gone. He got tired of being the punchline and decided to blend in with the crowd. He became louder, bolder, and dismissive towards those who were getting picked on. But here's the real deal: I knew this wasn't him. When it was just us or our crew, he was his usual self. But when he was around others, he turned into a different guy.

We eventually called him out on this change, this back-and-forth between who he really was and who he thought others wanted him to be. He was taken aback; he hadn't even noticed he was doing it, and it had become his norm. After we called him out, he started paying more attention and started fixing his behavior. He realized that while he couldn't control others' jokes, he had to make a choice about his own reactions. In the end, he made a conscious decision to spend less time with them and refocus his energy to align with his authentic self.

It's important to note that the Hyena Mask is a common facade for men wrestling with insecurities. It's often used by men who are desperately trying to fit in with the group, even if it means divorcing their true selves. They might resort to making fun of others or acting cruelly to feel better about themselves and to feel more accepted by the group. But this often leads to a feeling of emptiness and dissatisfaction because they aren't being true to themselves. Any mask, and especially the Hyena Mask, is a quick fix for deeper issues of insecurity. If you're wearing it, it's time to take a good look at yourself and face those underlying issues. Only then can you find true happiness and satisfaction.

So, let's look at the Hyena Mask more closely, scrutinize its traits, what it means, and the journey to unmasking. The Hyena Mask thrives on adaptation and impersonation, trying to fit into the undercurrents of the pack. However, it's crucial to remember that the pursuit of acceptance should never entail sacrificing one's individuality or personal integrity.

Take, for instance, the guy who becomes the life of the party, not because he genuinely enjoys the atmosphere but to draw attention away from his feelings of inadequacy or loneliness. He laughs the loudest, cracks the most jokes, and maybe even becomes the clown, all to avoid any potential ridicule or criticism. Or consider the guy who constantly changes his beliefs and opinions, not out of thoughtful consideration, but because he fears isolation or disagreement.

This Hyena Mask not only disguises the wearer's true emotions and thoughts but also reinforces negative behaviors such as bullying or mockery. By doing so, it feeds a vicious cycle where acceptance is earned through ridicule and self-suppression.

My childhood friend eventually made a conscious choice to take off his Hyena Mask, reevaluating his friendships and re-centering his focus on his genuine self. It was a hard decision, but it was necessary for his peace and authenticity.

It's time to realize that the Hyena Mask, though it may feel protective, is merely a disguise for deeper issues. If you find yourself in this mask, it's time to confront the real issues, unmask, and start the journey toward self-acceptance and authenticity. We, as men, can support each other through this process, holding each other accountable and fostering environments of acceptance, respect, and genuine camaraderie.

Let's say no to the Hyena Mask, break the cycle of self-suppression and external validation, and say yes to our authentic selves. Because that is where true happiness, fulfillment, and satisfaction lie.

1. CHARACTERISTICS OF THE HYENA MASK

Conformity: Men with the Hyena mask constantly agree with the majority, often going against their own beliefs or values for fear of being singled out or ridiculed. They find comfort in fitting in with the crowd, even if it compromises their individuality.

Adaptive Personality: These men adjust their behavior, attitudes, and even interests based on the company they keep. They become what they think others want them to be, often suppressing their own personality.

Fear of Rejection: The driving force behind the Hyena mask is often the fear of rejection or the need for acceptance. These men crave social approval and go to great lengths to avoid confrontation or disagreement.

2. IMPLICATIONS OF THE HYENA MASK

Loss of Self-Identity: Constantly conforming to societal expectations often leads to a loss of self-identity. The individual might struggle to recognize his own desires, beliefs, or values, as they are continually suppressed.

Inauthentic Relationships: The relationships formed while wearing the Hyena mask might be superficial or inauthentic, as they're based on a façade rather than the true self.

Psychological Struggles: The continual conflict between the real self and the façade can lead to psychological struggles, including stress, anxiety, and feelings of loneliness.

3. REMOVING THE HYENA MASK

Self-Reflection: Identifying and acknowledging the use of the Hyena mask is the first step toward removing it. It's important to evaluate situations where one feels the need to conform excessively and understand the reasons behind this need.

Develop Self-Confidence: Building self-confidence helps in expressing one's own thoughts and opinions without fear of rejection or ridicule. This can be achieved through self-affirmations, skill-building, and achieving small personal goals.

Find a Supportive Environment: Surrounding oneself with people who appreciate individuality and encourage self-expression can significantly ease the process of removing the Hyena mask.

Seek Professional Help: If the struggle with the Hyena mask causes significant distress, seeking professional help from a counselor or therapist can provide the necessary tools to manage and overcome these issues.

THE TURTLE MASK

In the beautiful dance of life, Leah and I have learned how to keep the beat within the rhythm, despite our contrasting styles. She leans towards a more analytical approach, weighing options, analyzing scenarios, and meticulously crafting plans. I, on the other hand, am more inclined to fly by the seat of my pants, preferring to jump in and figure things out along the way. These differences, rather than clashing, create a beautiful balance like the perfect mix of sweet and savory in a meal, with each flavor enhancing the other.

Admittedly, there was a time when our contrasting styles seemed less like a balanced dish and more like two opposing flavors that should be served separately. During our "deep talks" and what my friend Words Taylor would refer to as "Intense Fellowships", I often felt unheard and misunderstood. Instead of holding my ground and addressing the issue at hand, I'd automatically retreat into my thoughts and emotionally disconnect from the situation. If our conversation started to feel too heated or argumentative, I'd simply shut down. This response frustrated Leah, who was keen on resolving our issues immediately, while I preferred taking time to process them.

From Leah's perspective, we were having a dialogue, attempting to smooth over our differences and misunderstandings. However, I would respond by abruptly ending the discussion, resorting to silence, or patronizing her. Initially, my instinct to retreat and don my "Turtle Mask" was unconscious. But over time, this defensive mechanism became a conscious choice. Every time things got too chaotic or contentious, I'd withdraw into my shell. This retreat, while providing me temporary refuge, also served as self-imposed isolation, preventing me from connecting with Leah, who was only trying to understand and support me.

Whenever I approached her with an idea, she'd volley back with a barrage of questions. I now understand that she was simply trying to comprehend my thoughts, calculate potential risks, and come up with a well-rounded plan. However, at the time, all I felt was criticism and rejection. I misunderstood her cautious curiosity for attempts to dampen my enthusiasm, mistakenly labeling her a 'dream killer' instead of the supportive partner she truly was.

It wasn't until our relationship faced a serious setback that forced us to have difficult discussions, did I begin to see things differently. We recognized that we were two pieces of a puzzle – my spontaneity complementing her thoughtfulness. Leah was not there to dismantle my dreams, but to fortify them, to ensure their sustainability, and our mutual success. As this realization dawned on me, I began to discard my Turtle Mask, understanding that the path to resolution was open communication, not silent withdrawal. I had to reframe my perception of disagreements, recognizing them as necessary discussions rather than confrontations. Once I started sharing my frustrations and addressing miscommunications, I realized that the shell I had constructed was isolating me, and our contrasting approaches, which I assumed were pulling us apart, were in fact our collective strength when understood and appreciated.

Fast forward to the present, our relationship is stronger and more vibrant than ever. We've learned to value each other's unique qualities, and our combined strengths have reinforced both our personal relationship and our professional partnership.

The masks we wear – the Lion, the Hyena, or the Turtle, are not representations of our authentic selves. These are merely defensive shields we adopt in the hope of protection, often inadvertently leading to further isolation. Each mask comes with its own set of challenges. The Turtle mask, while offering a temporary refuge, can also foster solitude and emotional detachment. Self-reliance and independence are indeed virtues to be celebrated, but not at the expense of our emotional well-being or our relationships. My experience with the Turtle mask taught me three essential lessons: 1. Silence is not the solution, 2. Disagreements are not necessarily arguments, and 3. Questions from my wife do not imply doubt in my capabilities.

The Turtle mask provided me with a safe retreat during challenging discussions, but it also created a wall of solitude that disconnected me emotionally from my partner. Retreating into my shell might have helped me dodge the immediate discomfort of a heated conversation, but it also deprived us both of the opportunity to understand and come to the resolution we needed. It was when I learned to break through this shell and foster open dialogue that I truly began to appreciate our differences as strengths rather than obstacles.

Even more importantly, I began to understand that disagreements were not necessarily hostile arguments but necessary discussions that allowed us to understand each other better. Seeing every point of contention as an argument had led me to avoid them, but in truth, avoiding them wasn't doing us any good. Once I started opening up and voicing my feelings, I realized that this shell I'd built was only isolating me, and our differences, which I thought were pulling us apart, were actually our strengths when embraced.

Perhaps the most significant revelation was understanding that my wife's queries were not meant to quash my ideas but to strengthen them. She wasn't challenging my dreams but challenging the strategy and implementation. Her meticulous nature and tendency to ask questions were not a sign of disbelief in my abilities but an effort to support me and ensure our mutual success.

Today, we have a relationship that is more potent and harmonious than ever before. We've learned to lean into each other's strengths and use them as our superpowers, strengthening not just our personal bond but also our business partnership. My journey of discarding the Turtle mask has been a profound lesson in understanding that our masks are not our true selves. They are temporary armors that we believe will protect us, but in reality, they often isolate us further. Removing these masks is essential to open ourselves to real connection, authentic living, and true happiness.

BREAKDOWN: Turtle masks in-depth, examining their characteristics, implications, and the path to removing them:

Characteristics:
1. **Isolation:** Men wearing the Turtle Mask often prefer solitude and avoid social interaction. They may seem introverted or antisocial at that time.
2. **Suppression of Emotion:** The tendency to suppress their

emotions, hiding their feelings even from themselves. This can often be mistaken for calmness or stoicism.

3. **Avoidance of Conflict**: They avoid confrontations, arguments, and disagreements, often to maintain peace or to prevent emotional exposure.
4. **Dependency on Routine**: They can be overly dependent on routine or familiar settings, as these provide a sense of security.
5. **Overthinking**: Men with the Turtle Mask are prone to overthinking, reflecting on past events, or worrying about future possibilities.

Implications:

1. **Emotional Disconnection**: By suppressing their emotions, they disconnect themselves from their own feelings, leading to problems with emotional recognition and expression.
2. **Relationship Struggles**: Their tendency to avoid social interactions and conflicts can lead to strained relationships and difficulty forming new connections.
3. **Mental Health**: The lack of emotional expression, coupled with isolation, can contribute to mental health issues like depression and anxiety.
4. **Stunted Personal Growth**: By avoiding new experiences or challenges, they may limit their personal growth and self-development.

How to Remove the Turtle Mask:

1. **Acknowledge and Accept**: The first step is recognizing and accepting that the mask exists. Denial only strengthens its hold.
2. **Communicate:** Begin expressing your emotions and sharing your feelings with trusted individuals in your life. This could be friends, family, or professional therapists.
3. **Belief System:** Adjust your mindset to understand that when people disagree with you or question your choices, they aren't rejecting you. Whether it's a fresh innovative idea you're excited about or a decision you're considering, their questions aren't opposition. They're striving to understand your vision more deeply.
4. **Embrace Vulnerability**: Understand that showing emotions is not a sign of weakness but a demonstration of strength.

THE DOG MASK

As we dig deeper into our exploration of the mask's men wear, we now confront the Dog mask. Unlike the Lion, Hyena, and Turtle, the Dog mask represents a different kind of challenge. This mask embodies a man's desire for conquest and domination, especially in the realm of romantic and sexual relationships. The man wearing the Dog mask is often portrayed as a macho figure, asserting his perceived masculinity through promiscuity. He views women to be conquered and trophies to be won, validating his ego and providing him with a false sense of superiority. He equates quantity and bagging the baddest woman with success, his self-worth often measured by the number of his romantic conquests. However, this promiscuous lifestyle and view of relationships are far from being a sign of true confidence or masculinity and often reveal deeper insecurities. It is the reflection of a misguided belief that equates male worth to sexual conquering, a perspective reinforced by societal stereotypes and media portrayals. The Dog mask's implications are indeed detrimental, not only for the man himself but for his relationships and the women he interacts with.

A vivid flashback from my younger years paints a picture of my brothers rolling from one town to the next, their focus set on one pursuit: women. Their goal wasn't about finding a lifelong partner or a meaningful connection, but rather to add another victory to their tally. This influence, over time, subtly trained me to see women more as objects to be won, and less as individuals. Despite the profound respect I held for the women in my family, this skewed view quietly wormed its way into my perspective, making me see women as conquests rather than equals. The dynamics between my parents further bolstered my skewed understanding of relationships. Despite my father's love for my mother — a love I firmly believe existed — he never married her, even after nearly 50 years of togetherness. This scenario unconsciously set a complex precedent for me and my siblings to emulate. My father's recurrent betrayals and numerous offspring were a conundrum to my young mind. The affection I knew he held for my mother starkly contrasted his actions, which served as an unwelcome framework, shaping my understanding of a man's role within relationships.

As I navigated into adulthood and met my wife, I found myself attempting to replicate the dynamic I'd witnessed between my parents. My understanding of relationships was built on an unsteady foundation of casual encounters and exchanges rather than deep emotional connections. However, my wife, who came from a background where marriage was a cornerstone, helped bring perspective to my distorted viewpoint.

My college years, fortified by my father's misguided advice to conquer as many women as possible," served to reinforce the Dog mask that was beginning to harden around my identity. The prevalent culture, amplified by the locker-room banter about body count and conquests, created a toxic environment where many of us felt a pressure to participate in this relentless pursuit. While wrestling with my insecurities, I managed to mask them behind my athletic prowess, my role as a college football player, and my unique east coast flair that seemed appealing in the Midwest. This facade, woven with threads of the Dog mask, served as my armor, enabling connections with numerous women in the hope of finding validation and an escape from my reality.

This problem is further compounded by societal norms that seem to laud this toxic machismo, this incessant need to 'hunt and gather.' Phrases like 'men are dogs' often get thrown around so much so that some men begin to internalize this idea, consequently manifesting the behavior. If men took on the responsibility of holding one another accountable, we might begin to see a shift in these destructive patterns. I have personally experienced the transformative power of such accountability from my friends, which led me to introspect and make crucial behavioral changes. This confirms that we can challenge each other's belief systems, leading to healthier practices.

Moreover, the omnipresent influence of media and technology in our times presents another layer of complexity. Our screens are constantly flooded with sexualized content that further perpetuates the Dog mask. Young boys, fueled by their innate curiosity and exposure to such materials, risk normalizing this skewed view of relationships

66

and sexuality. It is our duty as parents to intervene and guide them through these influences.

This intervention requires open and non-judgmental conversations about sex, imbued with empathy. Our task is to provide a balanced narrative that helps our children make sense of what they've been exposed to. By guiding my son through his journey of discovery, I aim to disrupt this cyclical pattern, hoping to set a healthier example not only for him but for others as well. It's crucial that we comprehend the roots of this Dog mask. Its origins might seem innocent enough, disguised as youthful exploration or locker room banter, but these are the steppingstones on a path that devalues women and reduces them to mere objects. The narrative needs to change, and it starts with challenging and dismantling the Dog mask.

BREAKDOWN: Characteristics of the Dog Mask This mask is a symbol of a man's craving for dominance, particularly in the sphere of romantic and sexual relationships.

CHARACTERISTICS:

1. Asserts his masculinity through promiscuity, viewing women as conquests and trophies to be won.
2. Ties his self-worth to the number of romantic encounters he's had or the attractiveness of his partners.
3. Projects a macho image, aiming to embody societal expectations of "manliness".
4. Finds validation and a sense of superiority in his ability to charm and engage with multiple women.
5. Internalizes societal norms and phrases like "men are dogs,"

which perpetuates the cycle.

6. Often hides deep-seated insecurities behind this mask, seeking validation externally instead of confronting internal issues.

IMPLICATIONS OF THE DOG MASK: The implications of the Dog mask are severe, impacting not only the individual but also his relationships and interactions with women. They include:

1. The degradation and objectification of women, reducing them to mere trophies or conquests.
2. The reinforcement of toxic societal norms and expectations of masculinity.
3. A disconnect from meaningful relationships and genuine emotional connections, focusing instead on superficial, fleeting encounters.
4. The avoidance of confronting personal insecurities and weaknesses leads to the stagnation of personal growth.
5. Promoting a culture that validates this behavior, affects younger generations who may start to believe that this is what masculinity entails.

REMOVING THE DOG MASK: Removing the Dog mask involves introspection, accountability, and a change in mindset. Here are some steps to take:

1. **Acknowledge the Mask:** The first step is to acknowledge that you're wearing this mask and understand why you put it on in the first place. Dig deep into your insecurities and the societal norms that encouraged you to wear this mask.

2. **Introspection and Self-Reflection:** Reflect on how this mask has affected your life, relationships, and perception of women. Recognize the damage it may have caused and the implications it has on your well-being and growth.

3. **Challenge Societal Norms:** Question societal norms and expectations that glorify this behavior. Understand that these societal standards are often baseless and contribute to toxic masculinity.

4. **Promote Accountability:** Hold yourself and others accountable for this behavior. Openly discuss these issues with friends and family, encouraging them to challenge these norms as well.

5. **Engage in Open Conversations:** Start conversations about respect and consent and understanding women's perspectives and experiences. This could help reframe your understanding of relationships.

6. **Seek Therapy or Counseling:** If you find it challenging to remove the mask, don't hesitate to seek professional help. Therapists and counselors can provide valuable insights and coping mechanisms to help you navigate through this process.

By comprehending the deep-seated reasons behind the adoption of the Dog mask, we can take steps to remove it and foster healthier views of masculinity, relationships, and self-worth.

THE CHAMELEON MASK

You see, the Chameleon mask is very unique. While the wearer of this mask may be a master of fitting in, seamlessly flowing from one group to another, this ever-changing color can often result in a loss of self. These are the men who mold their thoughts and beliefs to fit the narrative of the company they keep, valuing harmony over authenticity.

This mask often emerges from a deep-seated fear of rejection. A Chameleon fears being left out or considered an outsider. So, he morphs, changes, bends, and twists to become the ideal version that he believes others want him to be. He seeks to please everyone, agreeing with popular opinions even when they contrast with his own, fearing that his authentic thoughts might lead to conflict or alienation. Yet, this constant adaptation comes at a heavy cost. At its core, the Chameleon mask results in a profound loss of authenticity. The man behind the mask might start to forget who he is as his identity becomes fluid and unstable, defined by external factors rather than an internal, unshakeable sense of self.

This mask not only impacts the wearer's personal sense of identity but also seeps into his relationships. When someone is perpetually shifting their beliefs and values to match their company, it becomes challenging to build deep and meaningful connections. This can be especially detrimental when it comes to fatherhood. Children need and want consistency, stability, and honesty, all of which become difficult to provide when one's identity is as changeable as a Chameleon's.

But here's the good news: we can shed this mask. The journey begins with self-awareness and acceptance. Recognize that you're wearing the Chameleon mask, and more importantly, acknowledge the implications. It's about accepting who you are at your core, without the need for external validation, and embracing your individuality. There is an unmatched power in being authentic being able to stand alone, in expressing an opinion that may not align with the crowd. Authenticity breeds respect, and it's okay to be the lone voice sometimes.

It's really important to work on developing meaningful, authentic relationships that are built on mutual respect for each other's individuality. Surrounding yourself with people who encourage you to be your true self, who love and respect you, Chameleon mask and all. Building emotional resilience is also key to shedding this mask. It's about understanding that rejection or isolation doesn't define your worth. Not everyone needs to like you or agree with you, and that's okay. It's better to be disliked for who you are than to be liked for who you are not. Recognizing this fundamental truth is crucial, especially when it comes to relationships. Too often, men compromise their authentic selves to fit into a persona that they believe would be more appealing to their partners.

In relationships, the Chameleon mask can create a unique set of challenges. In his quest to impress and please, a man wearing this mask might morph his interests, beliefs, or behaviors to align with those of the woman he's interested in. This is cool initially; however, this might seem charming and create the illusion of compatibility. Over time, this lack of authenticity can lead to disillusionment. If a man continually changes his colors to please his partner, she might feel like she's in a relationship with a mirage rather than a real person. It might also create insecurity in the man, as he constantly questions whether he is loved for who he truly is or for the version he portrays.

Similarly, in marriage or long-term relationships, the Chameleon mask can pose significant issues. As the chameleon continues to adapt, his spouse might feel lost, unsure of who their partner truly is. This can lead to trust issues, miscommunication, and emotional disconnect. The spouse may find it hard to confide in or rely on someone who is consistently changing. For the relationship to thrive, it's essential for both parties to be their authentic selves.

The Chameleon mask can also impact a man's work life, particularly his relationship with his supervisor. If he's always agreeing and never asserting his opinions for fear of disapproval, he may stunt his professional growth. Supervisors appreciate employees who bring fresh ideas and different perspectives to the table, not just nod in agreement. While diplomacy and tact are valuable traits in the workplace, they shouldn't come at the cost of one's authenticity and innovative thinking.

Yet, it's important to acknowledge that there are positive aspects to the Chameleon mask as well. The ability to adapt to various situations and groups can be a great strength, enhancing a man's social skills and making him more relatable. Being empathetic, flexible, and approachable are valuable traits in both personal and professional life. However, it's crucial to find a balance. Adaptability shouldn't mean losing one's sense of self. When a man can adjust to different environments while staying true to his core values and beliefs, he utilizes the positive aspects of the Chameleon mask without being restricted by it.

Shedding the Chameleon mask isn't about losing this ability to adapt; instead, it's about ensuring this adaptability doesn't overshadow one's authenticity. It's about learning to be true to oneself, even when the colors of the environment change. It's about understanding that fitting in isn't always as important as standing out for who you truly are.

BREAKDOWN: Men wearing the Chameleon mask are masters of adaptation. However, this knack for blending in isn't necessarily an asset, as it may seem on the surface.

CHARACTERISTICS:

1. **Conformity Over Authenticity**: Men under the Chameleon mask prioritize fitting in over staying true to their values. They may compromise their beliefs or suppress their true feelings to be accepted by the group they're in.

2. **Lack of a Solid Identity**: Their personal identity is fluid and unstable, constantly shaped by their environment, the people around them, or the circumstances they find themselves in. Their identity can appear entirely different depending on who they're with.

3. **Fear of Rejection**: At the heart of this mask often lies an intense fear of rejection or being left out. This fear fuels their need to constantly adapt and change to fit in, even at the cost of their authenticity.

4. **The Ever-Pleasing Persona**: They often strive to please others, frequently agreeing with popular opinion, even when it clashes with their own viewpoints. They fear that expressing their true thoughts might lead to conflict or alienation.

IMPLICATIONS OF THE CHAMELEON MASK:

The Chameleon mask has significant implications, affecting not only the individual but also his relationships and his role as a father:

1. **Loss of Authenticity**: Constantly changing colors to fit in leads to a loss of personal authenticity. Over time, they may forget who they truly are, struggling to define their identity outside of societal expectations or the company they keep.

2. **Compromised Relationships**: Relationships, both romantic and platonic, can suffer due to this lack of authenticity. It's difficult to build deep, meaningful connections when one isn't being genuine.

3. **Conflicting Values in Fatherhood**: This lack of a solid identity can be detrimental in fatherhood. Kids need stability and consistency, which can be challenging to provide when one's values and behaviors are continuously shifting.

REMOVING THE CHAMELEON MASK:

Here's how we can start peeling off the Chameleon mask:

1. **Self-Awareness and Acceptance**: Start by acknowledging the mask and its implications. Begin accepting who you are at your core, irrespective of external validations.

2. **Embrace Individuality**: Understand that it's okay to stand out, to have an opinion that may not align with the popular view. Embrace your individuality and learn to celebrate it instead of suppressing it.

3. **Build Authentic Relationships**: Foster relationships that

encourage authenticity and accept you for who you truly are. Surrounding yourself with such positive influences will lessen the need to blend in constantly.

4. **Develop Emotional Resilience**: Build resilience against the fear of rejection or isolation. Understand that not everyone needs to like or agree with you, and that's perfectly okay.

5. **Therapy or Counseling**: Consider seeking professional help if the journey seems overwhelming. Therapists can provide strategies to reclaim your authentic self.

In terms of fatherhood, it's crucial to present a consistent and authentic self to your children. Our children learn by example, and a father who is secure in his identity, who doesn't shift colors with every new situation, offers strength, confidence, and stability in the child.

THE PANDA MASK:

The Panda mask represents a dichotomy: while it's traditionally symbolized by calmness, non-confrontational behavior, and a preference for predictability and routine, it can also represent a man who is more concerned with his exterior image than with the obligations and responsibilities of manhood. This man uses his physical attractiveness or superficial charm to attract partners, but often falls short when it comes to upholding his commitments.

In the wild, pandas are striking, with their distinctive black and white coloration making them one of nature's most recognizable creatures. Men who wear this aspect of the Panda mask may use their external appearance and charisma to draw attention and secure partners.

However, like the panda that prefers a solitary, peaceful existence, they might evade the hard work of relationship-building, shying away from the challenges and responsibilities that come with being a true partner. As fathers, these Panda men can be quite perplexing. They might be the cool dads, always fun to be around, always in vogue. They enjoy the fun part of parenting but struggle when it comes to discipline, guidance, and setting boundaries. They may avoid the less glamorous, tough aspects of fatherhood, an evasion that can impact their children's growth and development.

As partners, the Panda men are often the charmers, the ones who draw you in with their allure. They might make grand gestures and leave strong first impressions. But, as the relationship deepens and the need for genuine commitment and hard work arises, the Panda man's shortcomings become evident. He may struggle with long-term commitments, shy away from conflict resolution, or fail to communicate effectively. His focus on superficiality often overshadows the need for real emotional depth and connection in a relationship.

In the professional environment, Panda men can be the smooth talkers, the ones who know how to make a presentation sparkle or charm their way through a sales pitch. Yet when it comes to routine tasks or facing the grunt work, their commitment may waver. They might evade responsibilities, pass on tasks, or shy away from challenges, potentially stunting their professional growth.

The Panda mask thus underlines the implications of superficiality and irresponsibility in men's lives. It shows how relying solely on physical attractiveness, charm, or other external factors is insufficient and can lead to a lack of depth and commitment in various aspects of life. Shedding the Panda mask entails recognizing these issues and emphasizing responsibility, commitment, and a balance between appearance and substance.

While the external allure of the Panda mask may seem appealing, true manhood comes from honoring commitments, taking responsibility, and engaging in relationships and tasks with sincerity and depth. By focusing on these areas, men can move beyond the limitations of the Panda mask and step into a more balanced, authentic version of manhood.

PANDA MASK BREAKDOWN: This is a guise that some men wear, placing high emphasis on their physical appeal as a means of securing attention and validation, often to the detriment of their responsibilities and commitments. It represents a man who embodies the superficial aspects of manhood, focusing primarily on his appearance while overlooking the significant aspects of responsibility, commitment, and emotional depth.

CHARACTERISTICS:

1. **Superficial Charm:** Men wearing the Panda mask are often attractive, charismatic, and know how to make a strong first impression. They tend to rely heavily on their physical appeal and social magnetism to navigate relationships and situations.
2. **Shirking Responsibility:** Panda men may dodge hard work, evade responsibility, and shun tasks that require deep commitment and follow-through.

3. **Avoidance of Conflict:** They prefer a smooth, uncomplicated life and tend to avoid confrontations, difficult discussions, or challenging situations.

4. **Inconsistency:** While they may excel in the early stages of relationships or tasks when the going gets tough, their commitment often wavers.

5. **Image Conscious:** They place a high value on appearance, be it physical or social, and can be excessively concerned about what others think of them.

IMPLICATIONS OF THE PANDA MASK:

1. **Impacted Relationships:** The Panda man's avoidance of responsibility and conflict can lead to strained relationships, both personal and professional. His partners may feel let down by his lack of commitment and emotional depth.

2. **Stunted Growth:** The lack of resilience and avoidance of challenging situations can hinder personal and professional development.

3. **Misplaced Priorities:** By focusing on the exterior and neglecting the interior, Panda men can develop an unbalanced sense of self, which can lead to feelings of dissatisfaction and emptiness over time.

REMOVING THE PANDA MASK:

1. **Embrace Responsibility:** One of the first steps to removing the Panda mask is accepting and fulfilling responsibilities in all aspects of life, from personal relationships to professional commitments.

2. **Cultivate Depth:** Invest in personal growth and emotional intelligence. Learn to value internal qualities such as integrity, empathy, and resilience as much as external charm.

3. **Engage in Conflict Resolution:** Instead of avoiding disagreements or difficult situations, learn effective conflict resolution strategies. Recognize that disagreements and challenges are opportunities for growth and essential parts of life.

4. **Seek Balance:** Find a balance between appearance and substance. While there's nothing wrong with caring about one's physical appearance, it's essential to also cultivate and value internal qualities.

5. **Self-Reflection:** Regular introspection can be a powerful tool for understanding one's motivations and actions. Reflect on instances where the mask may have taken precedence and consider alternative approaches.

THE OWL MASK:

The Owl Mask is donned by the man who uses his intellectual prowess, education, or job position as a tool of power and control. He places a high premium on knowledge, qualifications, and status, often using them to create a sense of superiority or to intimidate others. This man believes that his academic achievements, professional standing, or acquired wisdom grant him the right to belittle those whom he perceives as less knowledgeable or accomplished. He wields his intelligence like a weapon, using it to create distance rather than to connect, to dominate rather than to collaborate.

As a father, the man wearing the Owl mask can be excessively demanding and unapproachable. He may push his children to meet high academic standards and may not be understanding or supportive when they struggle or fall short. His children might feel overwhelmed by his intellectual prowess, intimidated to ask questions or to express themselves freely for fear of ridicule or criticism.

In the context of romantic partnerships, the Owl mask can create a dynamic of intellectual dominance and emotional coldness. A man wearing this mask might belittle his partner's opinions or achievements, instilling self-doubt and eroding self-esteem. This behavior can lead to an unhealthy power imbalance in the relationship, making genuine connection, empathy, and mutual respect difficult to achieve.

In the workplace, the Owl mask can manifest as a condescending attitude toward colleagues, an unwillingness to delegate, or a tendency to hoard knowledge. Such individuals may not listen to others' ideas, focusing on asserting their intellectual superiority rather than fostering team collaboration. This behavior can be detrimental to team dynamics and overall productivity, creating a hostile work environment that discourages open communication and innovation.

Ironically, while the man in the Owl mask may seem confident and in control, this mask is often an armor against deep-seated insecurities. The need to constantly prove intellectual superiority and the fear of appearing less knowledgeable can create significant stress and anxiety. Moreover, by reducing himself and others to mere reflections of their accomplishments, he loses sight of the multifaceted nature of human identity.

This mask, like others, can be discarded, but it requires self-awareness, humility, and conscious change. It involves recognizing that knowledge and intelligence are tools for understanding, growth, and connection, not weapons for dominance and intimidation. It also means accepting that one's worth as a human being is not tied to academic achievements or professional success.

Acknowledging that everyone has something valuable to contribute, regardless of their education or position, is another crucial step. Treating others with respect and empathy, and promoting an environment of learning and collaboration, both at home and work, can go a long way in replacing intellectual arrogance with intellectual humility.

Finally, it's essential to address the underlying insecurities that often drive the need to wear the Owl mask. This may involve self-reflection, therapy, or supportive conversations with trusted friends or family members. The aim is to cultivate a sense of self-worth that is not contingent on being the most knowledgeable or accomplished person in the room, but rather on being a compassionate, open-minded, and respectful individual. Remember, everyone wears masks at times. It's part of being human. The key is recognizing when a mask is preventing authentic connection and personal growth and then having the courage to take it off. That's the journey from boyhood to manhood - not a straight line, but a winding path, full of bumps and turns. It's about taking one step at a time, knowing that each step, each stumble, brings us closer to our authentic selves. And it's this authenticity, this courage to be real, that helps to heal the broken boy within and allows the man to emerge.

THE BREAKDOWN: The Owl Mask represents a man who uses his knowledge, education, and intellectual prowess as a way to assert dominance and superiority over others. He hides behind his intellect, using it as a shield against vulnerability and a weapon to intimidate others. Often, he may seem unapproachable and excessively demanding, especially in relationships or parenthood, where he sets unrealistically high standards based on his intellectual expectations.

CHARACTERISTICS OF THE OWL MASK

1. **Intellectual Superiority**: The man wearing the Owl mask prizes intellect above all and uses it as a tool to assert dominance. He believes his knowledge and education make him superior to others.

2. **Intimidating Presence**: He often uses his education or knowledge as a shield and a weapon, intimidating others into submission or silence.

3. **Unapproachable**: This man tends to be unapproachable, creating a barrier with his intellectual prowess. He rarely shows vulnerability or invites open, genuine communication.

4. **Demanding**: In relationships and as a parent, the man behind the Owl mask sets excessively high standards, often pushing his partner or children to meet them, creating unnecessary stress and pressure.

IMPLICATIONS OF THE OWL MASK:

1. **Erosion of Self-Esteem in Others**: By asserting intellectual dominance, the man with the Owl mask can erode the self-esteem of those around him, particularly his children and romantic partner.

2. **Creates Unhealthy Dynamics**: This mask can create an unhealthy power imbalance in relationships and the workplace, causing stress, conflict, and a lack of collaboration.

3. **Loss of Authentic Connection**: Wearing the Owl mask can hinder the formation of genuine connections, as others may feel intimidated or belittled.

4. **Internal Stress and Insecurity**: Despite appearing confident, the man behind the Owl mask may harbor deep-seated insecurities. The constant need to prove his intellectual superiority can cause significant stress and anxiety.

REMOVING THE OWL MASK:

1. **Cultivate Humility**: Recognize that intelligence and education are not measures of human worth, and everyone has valuable insights and experiences to share.

2. **Promote a Collaborative Environment**: Encourage open communication, listening to others' ideas, and fostering a learning and collaborative environment in your personal and professional life.

3. **Practice Empathy and Respect**: Treat others with empathy and respect, acknowledging their feelings and ideas even if they differ from your own.

4. **Address Underlying Insecurities**: Seek help to address underlying insecurities that drive the need to wear the Owl mask. This could involve self-reflection, therapy, or conversations with trusted individuals.

5. **Teach and Inspire, Don't Intimidate**: Use knowledge and education to inspire and teach others rather than intimidate or belittle them.

Remember, removing the Owl mask isn't about diminishing your intellect or achievements, but rather about using them to connect, collaborate, and contribute positively to the lives of those around you.

As we bring this exploration of the masks that men wear to a close, it's crucial to recognize that every mask, whether it's the Lion, the Hyena, the Turtle, the Dog, the Chameleon, the Owl, or the Panda, serves as a shield of defense, a fortress built upon the foundations of fear, insecurity, societal expectations, or distorted self-perceptions. These masks, in their myriad forms, represent the various ways men conceal their authentic selves, choosing the facade of perceived strength over the vulnerability of genuine connection.

The Lion Mask shows us the dangers of suppressing our emotions and maintaining a rigid image of invincibility. The Hyena Mask illustrates the harm of using humor as a diversion to mask our pain, deflecting deep conversations and vulnerability. The Turtle Mask reveals the perils of retreating into our shells when faced with conflict or discomfort, demonstrating how avoidance can deteriorate relationships and obstruct personal growth.

With the Dog Mask, we understand the harm of defining masculinity by conquest, realizing that true strength doesn't lie in the number of romantic or sexual conquests, but in respect and mutual understanding. The Chameleon Mask shows us how constantly altering our identity to fit in can lead to a loss of our unique selves, impacting our integrity and authenticity.

The Owl mask underscores the damage that intellectual arrogance can cause, using knowledge not as a tool for empowerment, but as a weapon of intimidation. Lastly, the Panda Mask exposes the fallacy of relying solely on physical attractiveness to find self-worth, emphasizing that beauty is far more than just skin deep, and that neglecting responsibilities can lead to a hollow, unfulfilled life.

Each mask is a testament to the struggle many men face daily, battling societal expectations of what it means to be a 'real man'. But it's essential to understand that these masks are just that - masks. They're not who we truly are. As we begin to peel back the layers, we confront the vulnerabilities and fears we've been hiding. It's a difficult process, one that requires courage, self-reflection, and often, professional help. But the reward is the unburdened freedom of living authentically, the deepening of our relationships, and the ability to genuinely connect with others and ourselves.

In the journey of fatherhood, partnership, or simply being a man, these masks might seem like necessary armor. Still, in truth, they often cause more harm than protection. The challenge is not just recognizing these masks but also committing to removing them, one step at a time. As we unmask, we don't just grow as individuals, but we also set an example for others around us - our partners, friends, and children - showing them that it's okay to be vulnerable, it's okay to be authentic. Unmasking is not about exposing our weaknesses, but rather about reclaiming our true strength - our humanity.

Because when we remove our masks, we aren't broken men; we're just men, unbroken and unmasked, embracing the beautiful complexity of our humanity. Our boys learn from us, and it's up to us to demonstrate that it's okay to let go of these masks. After all, it is only when we break these cycles that we can hope for a future where boys grow up to be men who don't need to hide behind masks. The removal of each mask is not a loss, but a return to authenticity, a step towards a world where broken boys don't have to become broken men.

-4-
TOXIC MASCULINITY

In our society, we often treat the term "masculinity" as an immovable, fixed concept. It's that perceived ideal that our boys are expected to live up to—stoic, tough, and emotionless ideologies. We unconsciously arm them with a hard shell, a defense that portrays "Me against the world." But deep down, beneath this armored facade, they remain what they were all along—human, vulnerable, complex, and emotional.

It's critical to understand that masculinity isn't toxic by nature. The toxicity seeps in when it becomes restrictive, limiting our boys' wide emotional spectrum to anger and indifference. It's when the terms "man up" and "boys don't cry" become more than just phrases, transforming into an invisible, burdensome expectation.

We, the fathers, bear an important responsibility. We are the mirrors our sons look into, the molds that shape their understanding of what it means to be a man. But we can't let our reflections become a distorted image of suppressed emotions and unspoken traumas.

It's about time we redefine the traditional concept of masculinity, molding it into a more holistic, humanistic view that includes empathy, sensitivity, and open emotional expression, not suppression. We have to not only say it as men but model the behavior that says, "It's okay to feel, it's okay to hurt, and it's okay to express it!" These aren't signs of weakness but a badge of honor and strength.

One event that recently took over the world stage and shed light on the issue of toxic masculinity was the incident involving Will Smith and Chris Rock during an awards ceremony. This incident showcased the clash of two forms of masculinity in the public eye, unraveling in real-time and sparking heated debates across the globe.

Will Smith, a widely recognized actor, and Chris Rock, a famed comedian, were both participants and spectators in a theater filled with industry peers and millions of viewers. Chris Rock, known for his cutting humor, made a joke about Jada Pinkett-Smith, Will's wife, relating to her alopecia condition, a condition that causes hair loss.

Although a part of Chris Rock's comedic routine, the joke struck a deeply personal chord with Will Smith. It was not received lightly at his wife's expense, causing a momentary burst of anger from Smith, who walked up on stage and slapped Rock. It was a moment of raw emotion that took everyone by surprise.

From a societal perspective, one could interpret Will Smith's reaction as a defense mechanism, a demonstration of his manhood, and an act of protecting his wife. However, this is where the subtle aspects of toxic masculinity seep into the narrative. It's worth noting that Jada Pinkett-Smith herself, the subject of the joke, was originally seen laughing during the incident, and so was Smith. It wasn't until a few seconds later that Jada's facial expressions changed from humor to either sadness, hurt, or discontent. At that moment, Smith was seen exiting his seat and approached Chris Rock up on the stage. Smith's physical reaction can be seen as asserting dominance and control, projecting his anger physically rather than addressing it verbally or intellectually. Watching the incident unfold in real time was nothing short of startling. At first, it felt like a well-crafted prank or part of the scripted event, just as the rest of the world probably perceived it. But the illusion shattered when Will returned to his seat, continuing to hurl obscenities at Chris Rock. This incident personified toxic masculinity in an unexpected and high-profile setting, revealing the internal struggles many men grapple with.

Indeed, I have engaged with hundreds of men in prison and out of prison who have had their lives permanently altered by the choices they made in fleeting moments of anger or fear. The dilemma faced by Will Smith is a familiar one to many men: Should I keep my cool? Does being calm make me seem weak? I am scared, but showing fear could cost me respect that may be impossible to regain. Ultimately, a man might confront the issue head-on, potentially resulting in life-altering consequences.

Yet even for those who choose to walk away, the struggle does not end. Even though they might have avoided a regrettable situation, they may still be wrestling with perceived judgments from others. This struggle is particularly pronounced among both young boys and young men. However, this is something that grown adult men face as well, but if addressed properly in their youth, men will have a better chance to navigate such situations. As a society and as parents, we must become more aware of the messages we send verbally and non-verbally.

Often, we preach one thing while embodying something entirely different, leaving our young boys confused and unsure of how to react. When boys choose to walk away because they understand it's the best decision, we must be close enough to help them navigate the complex emotions they may be processing alone. That is something that I stress and prioritize in my personal relationship with my children. Otherwise, they may be too afraid to express their feelings because the decision to walk away, rather than empowering them, might have left them feeling diminished. This is a common yet overlooked mental maze that many men navigate alone when dealing with conflict.

Will seeing the pain in his wife's eyes contributed to him making the decision to resort to violence in a public setting, Smith unfortunately and later regrettably reinforced the problematic stereotype that men should respond to perceived threats or insults with aggression. This incident becomes a case study of the harmful aspects of traditional masculinity, where restraint and dialogue are sidelined for physical retaliation.

Moreover, the incident emphasizes the complex interplay between public reputation, ego, and emotional management for men in society. Will Smith, despite his public persona of composure and charisma, some may say he fell victim to the societal pressure that demands a man to be the overt protector, but at the end of the day he chose to not handle the situation with grace and conversation. I cannot say that it would have been easy to use restraint in that moment when you have millions of people watching, and your wife is looking at you in sadness. However, it is our responsibility as men to continue to do the internal work. It is also believed that his additional family affairs could have also contributed to his public outburst.

The incident shocked many, primarily because it challenged our understanding of both figures. It highlighted the toxicity latent in cultural expectations of masculinity. The aftermath left the audience divided, with some sympathizing with Smith's defense of his wife, while others criticized his lack of control, thus reinforcing the importance of having open conversations about healthy masculinity.

The Will Smith-Chris Rock incident provides a critical lens to view toxic masculinity, highlighting the dire need to redefine manhood in contemporary society, to dismantle the toxic behaviors often considered acceptable, and to engage in continuous dialogue to ensure respect and understanding between all genders.

MY SON WILL NOT SHOW SIGNS OF WEAKNESS

During one of my workshops, a concerned mother sought my advice. She detailed a complex situation in her home; she and her boyfriend were raising a son together and found herself at a crossroads. Each time her son exhibited emotion, showed fear, or behaved in any way perceived as not 'manly enough,' her boyfriend harshly chastised him, labeling him as 'soft' and accusing him of 'acting like a girl.'

Her dilemma centered on how to handle the reoccurring issue that she perceived as toxic behavior by her boyfriend. Regardless of the many conversations they had concerning this issue, she constantly faced opposition from the father of her child. Complicating matters was her upbringing - she had grown up with a single mother, without the influence of a positive male role model, and her father was conspicuously absent from her life. Consequently, she lacked a clear perspective on the correct conduct of a man and the nuances of fatherhood. Her boyfriend, the male figure in her household, was the one she was looking to for guidance, and she trusted that he would guide their son down the right path.

I explained to her that there's no one-size-fits-all solution. Every family, every situation, every individual is unique. Although I didn't agree with Dad, I understood the father's mindset, recognizing it as a product of deep-seated societal conditioning. If I were advising him directly, I'd want to explore the factors that triggered his discomfort whenever his son displayed emotions. What experiences from his own past, or ingrained belief systems, would drive him to suppress his son's emotional expression and indict him to a way of being based on his actions?

The root of Dad's thinking lies in his belief systems. I firmly believe that the bedrock of his response is deeply entrenched in his belief system surrounding masculinity. This powerful yet often invisible driver of our actions tends to be overlooked because it isn't something we can physically touch or see. Yet, it dictates how we behave and interact with the world. In many instances, including this one, toxic masculinity emerges as a manifestation of one's own belief systems. It supports numerous behaviors, particularly those linked to men who exert overbearing control or resort to aggression. What was Will's belief system in his situation? What did he believe? We have to intentionally look at our belief systems to begin to reshape the narrative and actions of toxic masculinity. As for the father, I could advise him on alternative approaches to responding to his son's emotions, but the real transformative work lies in challenging his fundamental beliefs and the father doing his internal work. This involves helping him reevaluate and reshape the deep-seated beliefs that might be anchored in possible past trauma.

Mom doubled down that she believes that he harbors deep-seated fears that their son might grow up to be gay or perceived as 'soft' or unable to cope with the world if he were to continue showing signs of vulnerability. This father's struggle is mirrored in countless other men who grapple with the delicate balance of raising boys. Wanting them to be manly, inclined in sports, jumping, wrestling, etc. Yet, their attempts to raise manly boys can sometimes lead to overcompensating, inadvertently inflicting more harm than good.

One of the most pervasive deceptions men are made to believe is that expressing emotion or showing vulnerability equates to weakness. This fear—that their sons, if they expose their emotions, will be perceived as weak, become targets, and lose their 'macho' image—is a widespread issue that shapes the parenting strategies of many fathers.

On a personal note, I, too, faced a similar challenge when my son Levi was a baby. I saw him playing with a doll at the daycare center. Seeing the shock on my face, one of the daycare workers approached me and helped me process the situation. She explained the nature of child development, emphasizing that my son's toy choice wasn't about gender norms but a part of his innocent exploration and learning. This interaction forced me to reassess my approach to parenting. I had to look within and make sure I was guiding and protecting my child, but not from a place of fear and toxicity. Based on my preconceived notions, I could have imposed restrictions on what my son could or couldn't do, but I chose instead to trust the daycare worker's expertise while focusing on my role as a father. This experience proved to be transformative, helping me grow as a parent and as a person. This allowed my son to explore, but with me present.

Remembering that our convictions as men can seep into and shape how we raise our children is imperative. We must stay vigilant of those moments that can potentially leave indelible marks. How a young father manages or suppresses his emotions can create a lasting impact, much like my experience with my son's playtime.

In essence, we must be both deliberate and present in navigating these defining moments. It's counterproductive to parent from a place of trauma or to adopt a "because I said so, and that's how it's always been done!" attitude. Instead, being fully present and mindful allows us to provide our children with the best possible tools for their future, ensuring they have a fair chance to thrive and grow. Think about it; think about how you were ignored or neglected. Think about the mishandled moments of our own fathers or father figures. We mustn't replicate what we experienced.

Merely being a male doesn't automatically translate into what it means to be a good man. A balanced, emotionally healthy man isn't about suppressing feelings; it's about understanding and managing them constructively. It's extremely important for us to redefine what strength means for men. Strength isn't just about physical power or dominance; it's about emotional intelligence, the ability to adapt, and the humility to learn from our mistakes.

THE YOUNGER VERSION OF ME

I think about the younger toxic version of myself that caused my family to experience financial devastation. My behavior was rooted in who was right rather than what was right. It was all about me and me getting my needs met. Money didn't motivate the path to our financial ruin at the time. It was me wanting to exercise my power, my perceived power. It was about living up to an antiquated and damaging model of masculinity that equates manhood with being right, tough, and in control. The thought of my wife managing our finances challenged my pride. Yep, I said it. My wife managed the money, and I struggled with that. I thought that because I was the man of the house, I made the most money; therefore, I should manage the house money. Foolish, all the way foolish in my thinking. How could a man with a 500-credit score think he should be managing the money? I'm not saying that you are incapable of managing the finances just because you have a bad credit score because life happens to us all. But in my case, I had the money and refused to pay my bills. I was extremely irresponsible. And so, for me to have an issue, it was my distorted view of masculinity. All I could see or think about was me relinquishing my role as the man of the house. I saw it as me losing control instead of having the best-qualified person operating in their gifting and assignment. What a toxic trait and mindset to have!

Eventually, I had to learn the hard way, bankruptcy. Although my wife managed the money, I kept her in the dark of some of my financial affairs and eventually self-sabotaged us. I had to acknowledge that my wife's strengths don't make me less of a man. In fact, it's a sign of strength when we embrace and support it. It took the failure of my business and a massive blow to my ego to understand this. And in the process, I realized I wasn't just impacting my own life; I was setting an example for my children and potentially perpetuating toxic and harmful stereotypes about what it means to be a man for them.

This is the message I want to pass on to my son and all the young men out there. Manhood isn't about never showing emotions or always having control. It's about respecting yourself and others, understanding your emotions, and working in harmony with those around you. It's about standing up for what's right, even when it's hard and even when it's against what society has told you a man should be. Toxic masculinity focuses on the self and not the whole. I was so worried about myself and my ego that I forgot about my family, role, and responsibility as a partner in my relationship with my wife and family. Writing this is still humbling. I can remember it all as if it were yesterday. I had to change the narrative around my masculinity for the sake of my son and daughters. I had to begin to build a world where my son can express his feelings without fear of being seen as less manly and where he can accept criticism and digress if someone is better suited or more qualified than him. See their superpowers as strengths without seeing them as threatening his manhood. I had to teach him that a man's worth isn't determined by how much money he makes or how many decisions he controls but by the content of his character.

BREAKING FREE

I recently encountered a father who joined my fatherhood group. This father was grappling with a heart-wrenching divorce and struggled to make sense of his situation. He privately told me how he lost his joy and purpose for living and was unmotivated. I encouraged him to meet with me one-on-one and that he would greatly benefit from attending our weekly group sessions with other men present. Initially, he struggled to share his story within the group, but like most men that attend our groups, they quickly find out that It's almost impossible not to express emotion or become vulnerable. He exploded like a volcano, a good volcano. He started to share his heart.

Initially, he carried a mindset where he viewed himself as without fault in the dissolvement of his marriage, placing the blame squarely on his wife. However, his perspective shifted as he allowed the men to speak into his life and help him process the events and moments in his marriage. As he became more integrated into the group, he shared more and more of himself. Prior to this happening, he stated that he never shared or opened up to a group of men as he has done with them. He stated that he was afraid and worried. Although he desired it and wanted it, the fear of ridicule and rejection was much more powerful than his becoming free. Not only did he become vulnerable, but he became so vulnerable that he shed tears and started to speak about the absence of his father and its pain.

Initially, the man was quick to point fingers at his wife, blaming her for all their marital woes. However, as he engaged in conversation and absorbed the insights from the group of men, he started to recognize his own role in their unraveling relationship. He realized that he had burdened her with unreasonable expectations. He had distanced himself from the faith that had once been the cornerstone of their partnership. His career had begun to take precedence over his family, and he had lost sight of prioritizing his marriage and family as essential rather than optional.

Moreover, he conceded that he grappled with deep-seated abandonment issues. This fear of loss lurked beneath the surface, acting as a constant reminder of potential disaster. He was perpetually braced for his comfortable life to take a downward turn, always hanging on the precipice of catastrophe. Whether it involved his marriage, career, personal relationships, or health, he could never fully savor the good moments due to his preparedness for the worst.

So, when the divorce eventually occurred, his mindset reflexively went, "See, I knew this was coming. This is what I was expecting. This is normal." His persistent anticipation of disaster had deprived him of truly appreciating the positive aspects of his life.

Their accountability and support offered him perspectives that challenged his initial view of his wife and found solace and another viewpoint on his situation. Most importantly, he became revitalized in his spirit. He went from feeling dejected and unmotivated to setting goals and embracing life. He found joy in little things again, even laughing at commercials, symbolizing his newfound positivity. He acknowledged the importance of becoming transparent, taking accountability, and being open to growth.

In fostering a supportive and understanding environment, the fatherhood group gave him the platform he needed to vent his pent-up emotions. His transformation only came when he became open to the power of shared experiences and collective support in navigating the treacherous waters of personal crises. His opening up in a shared space knocked down his wall of toxic masculinity so that he cannot be vulnerable or share his thoughts and feelings with other men. The changes he experienced were a reflection of his willingness to embrace vulnerability, take responsibility, and embark on a growth path. Let me ask you a question, did his situation change? No, however, his disposition changed and his posture in accountability changed.

Toxic masculinity's influence permeates our lives, often in subtle ways that we might overlook until they reach a boiling point. The examples shared in this chapter, from the Oscars stage to the personal experiences of fathers struggling with how to raise emotionally intelligent sons, illustrate the pervasive and damaging effects of these societal expectations. The fear of vulnerability, the valorization of aggression, and the suppression of emotions can distort our understanding of manhood and lead to harmful behaviors. These stories also underscore the importance of self-awareness and personal growth in breaking the cycle of toxic masculinity. We need to challenge the age-old narratives about manhood that discourage men from acknowledging and expressing their emotions openly and healthily.

-5-
THROUGH HIS EYES

There's a strange paradox that exists in life: sometimes, the very thing we crave is the very thing we run away from. Such was the case for me when it came to seeing people through God's eyes, a concept so challenging, it turned my world upside down. People yearn for understanding but shrink away from the discomfort it often brings. In the midst of my own emotional turmoil, the last thing I wanted was to look at the ones who caused me pain through the lens of Christ. My heart ached, throbbing with the echoes of my past, yearning for retribution rather than reconciliation. It was all-consuming, blinding me to anything else, holding me captive in the chains of resentment and bitterness.

One evening, my wife and I found ourselves amidst the laughter and warmth of a dinner shared with friends. As we swapped stories of trials and triumphs, our companions introduced us to a practice that had helped sustain their marriage – seeing each other through God's eyes. Their words resonated within me, striking a chord that played an unfamiliar yet captivating melody. It was during this conversation, enveloped in the comfort of companionship, that I confronted the profound concept they had learned from their own struggles.

Their words painted a vivid image – looking at your partner not through the distorted lens of human imperfection but through God's eyes, seeing them in the light of love, compassion, and potential. Suddenly, the flaws and failings that dominated your vision dissipate, replaced by their inherent worth as God's creation. A simple shift in perspective, yet monumental in its implications.

I wish I could tell you that this revelation was a magic bullet, instantly mending my wounds and altering my perspective. However, that was far from the truth. I wrestled with this new-found wisdom, grappling with old grudges that clung stubbornly to my spirit, particularly my fraught relationship with my father.

The relationship I shared with my father wasn't bathed in the warm light of love, but it was more an eclipse – a dark shadow cast over my childhood. His love wasn't the warm, comforting kind that children crave. It was cold, distant, and occasionally harsh. My childhood memories were marred by his unkindness, and it felt like an insurmountable task to try and view him through God's compassionate lens.

A memory etched in my heart came back to me then. I was eight years old, standing by the roadside with my mother, our lives packed into a few suitcases. My mother, displaying a boldness I hadn't seen before, confided in me that we were leaving my father. My young mind couldn't comprehend the gravity of the situation. All I knew was a primal fear of losing access to my father. Tears streaming down my face, I begged my mother not to leave. Touched by my pleas, she decided to stay, remaining in an unfulfilling relationship for almost 50 years.

As I grew older, anger started to brew within me, simmering beneath the surface. I witnessed the pain etched on my mother's face, the regret that filled her eyes whenever she recalled that fateful day. Her dream of a loving marriage remained unfulfilled, and I felt overwhelming guilt, blaming myself for having made her stay. I harbored resentment against my father, a bitter pill that tainted our already strained relationship.

Struggling with these raw, powerful emotions, I was challenged to see my father - the man I held responsible for our familial hardships - through God's eyes. A journey I knew was necessary, but equally daunting. Through His Eyes, a chapter of my life was about to unfold. It was a path to understanding, forgiveness, and ultimately, healing. It required me to put aside my anger, my resentment, my pain, and try to see the man who had caused me so much hurt, through the eyes of love, compassion, and divine potential.

In time, I rose from my struggles, battered but not broken, and I found my calling in football. I became good at it, remarkably good. Accolades and recognition followed me across the country. The irony was not lost on me, that the same father who told me I was too small to play the sport was now parading around the city, proudly proclaiming that I was his son. He even asked my mother to change my last name from Hart to his own, Burns. But the choice was mine, not his, and it was not one I was ready to make lightly.

At the time when my father asked, I was seventeen, no longer afraid of him, and had a chip on my shoulder. I decided to keep my mother's last name. The disappointment on his face, the hurt and sadness, was a victory for me. I was finally in control.

However, despite the resentment, I also began to realize the importance of forgiveness. My mother, despite the pain she endured at his hands, would tell me that I need to find a way to forgive him. She believed forgiveness was a path towards healing.

In the last days of my mother's life, she again urged me to reconcile with my father. And so, I began to work on it, though I was still filled with anger. The process involved having a one-on-one conversation with my father, where I could ask him all the questions that had been weighing on my heart. Why did he never marry my mother? Why did he treat me the way he did? How did he feel about his own father?

This conversation provided closure and relief. My father's answers revealed to me that he was doing the best that he knew how to do, with the resources he had. The realization didn't erase my pain, but it gave me perspective. I began to see my father as a victim of his own circumstances. The little boy who was neglected, the man who felt abandoned, the father who was absent from his own family.

I was grateful for this chance to reconcile with my father, as now he is in the later stages of dementia. If I had waited, I would not have been able to get the answers I needed.

So, I want to convey a message to you, regardless of whether your father is living or not. Today is the day you start restoring relationships. You need to close that door, to move on without the burden of resentment. To heal, you must begin seeing the person who hurt you, the person who took advantage of you, through the eyes of God. It's not about absolving them of their wrongdoing. It's about freeing yourself from the pain and the trauma. It's about understanding the circumstances that led them to hurt you.

Healing is a process. When I first thought I had forgiven my father, my wife pointed out that I was still acting out of resentment. I had to accept that I was not completely healed. But when I truly desired to forgive him, that's when I started making progress. I had to let God wreck me and reshape me from the inside out so that I could become a better man, a better husband, and a better father.

With God as my lens, I managed to find forgiveness for the man who stole my brother from this world. The journey was steep, filled with countless hurdles and moments of self-reflection. Over time, it became clear that the resentment I harbored was only shackling me in my own torment. I reached out to him, our words exchanged through emails, and in the act of forgiving, I found a sense of liberation and inner strength. This bores witness to the profound healing found when one views others through the compassionate lens of Gods eyes.

What follows is the email I sent to him. Remember, this was less about him and more about my journey of healing, about learning to view those who have caused me pain through God's merciful gaze.

From: Shon Hart

Date: 10/24/2018 8:31:29 AM

Sent To: ███████████████

Attachments:

Hi sir,

You do not know me. I wanted to send you this letter for years but was unable to do it. However, I have found enough strength to send this letter to you. My name is Shon Hart and I am the younger brother of Travis Burns.

I am sending you this letter to tell you that I forgive you for what you've done. It was hard getting past the loss of my brother, but as a man I understand and owe it to you and to God to forgive you.

I pray that you are a changed man and that you love everyday and moment making a difference. I pray that you've forgiven yourself of the act you've committed.

My dad is still having a hard time dealing with it and I continually encourage him to find out in his heart to forgive, but he is unable to at this time. But, Cecil I need you to know that I forgive you and hold no malice toward you.

God bless

After sending the letter, I found myself wrapped in an incomprehensible blend of emotions. There was a sense of relief like a massive weight had been lifted off my chest. But there was also fear, the fear of not knowing how he would react, or if he would even read my words. I also felt like I had betrayed my dad because he was still extremely angry and hurt and unable to forgive him for his senseless act against his child.

Writing that letter to the man who took my brother from me took everything I had. There were moments when the pain was so intense, the loss so profound, that I doubted whether I could finish. Every word I penned was a step taken through a battlefield, against the raw grief that sought to pull me back, to keep me locked in bitterness and anger.

But there was also an undercurrent of strength, a newfound resilience born from the depths of despair. As the words poured out, each sentence became a testament to the strength of the human spirit and the capacity we hold for forgiveness, even in the face of unfathomable loss. And employing the "Through His Eyes." Concept.

Seeing him through His eyes, I learned, was not just about ManMan (*his name is not ManMan, I will use it for this purpose only*) —it was about me too. It was about liberating myself from the chains of hatred and resentment that threatened to consume me. It was about allowing myself to heal, to find peace, even amidst the storm, and see ManMan through his eyes.

There was a strange kind of tranquility after I hit send. As if the storm had washed away the grime, leaving only the raw, unblemished reality behind: I had done what I set out to do. I had found it in my heart to start the process.

In doing so, I had not excused ManMan for what he did, nor had I forgotten. I had simply chosen to no longer allow this event to hold dominion over me.

What happened next was incredible. ManMan responded and was very remorseful, and offered to sit down with me and answer any questions I may have had. I took him up on his offer and we made plans to connect in December of 2022, however, he was not released from prison. So, we decided to postpone our meetup until he is physically released from prison. He was given 30 - 50 years. My father may one day find it in his heart to forgive, or he may not. I don't know and the last time we talked it was a sensitive subject.

This is a chapter of my life that is now written, not with a period, but with a comma. As the story continues, my journey of healing carries on, and as the author of my life, I will continue to strive towards love, understanding, and most importantly, towards peace.

Because at the end of the day, I have learned that seeing people through His eyes is not a destination, but a journey. A journey that has taught me the strength of vulnerability, the power of compassion, and the transformative potential of forgiveness.

I learned that forgiveness doesn't always come with grand gestures or eloquent words. Sometimes it's an email to someone who some would say doesn't deserve forgiveness. Sometimes, it's a simple touch or a silent moment shared. My father and I never exchanged elaborate words of apology or forgiveness. One day, as he sat in his recliner, lost in the fog of dementia, I simply walked up to him, took his hand in mine, and said, "I forgive you, Dad." He looked up at me, his eyes welling with tears, his grip tightening on my hand. We shared a moment of understanding, a moment of healing, without any grand declarations.

In the years that followed, I worked hard to let go of the pain, resentment, and trauma. I invested my time and energy into building a loving family of my own, ensuring that my children never had to experience the abandonment I did. I became a successful football player, proving to myself and the world that the limitations imposed on me were not my reality. I became a public speaker, sharing my story to inspire others who might be going through similar circumstances.

I don't claim that my path was easy, or harder, or that anyone should walk the same one. What worked for me might not work for you. But

I do believe that forgiveness, understanding, and seeing others through the eyes of God can provide a path to healing. It can free us from the shackles of our past and help us create a better future.

My mother, my career, my faith, and my family have been my beacons of hope. They have taught me about strength, resilience, love, and the power of forgiveness. They helped me become the man I am today.

In life, it is not the pain or the trauma that defines us, but how we rise from them. It is about the lessons we learn and the strength we find within ourselves to forgive and move on.

This is the legacy I wish to leave behind, a legacy of hope, healing, and forgiveness. Not as a fatherhood practitioner, not as a public speaker, but as a man who found a way to rise above the pain, forgive those who hurt him, and build a life filled with love and compassion.

-6-
DEAR MA

In the grand tapestry of our existence, our mothers often hold an indelible imprint. They impart wisdom, provide guidance, and envelop us with love that helps mold our characters. It is crucial to convey to our mothers, be they physically present or residing in our memories, the significant impact they have had on our lives. Penning a letter to your mother creates an intimate space where you can express your sentiments of affection, thankfulness, and perhaps, longing.

This act is more than just a correspondence; it's a therapeutic journey to reconcile unresolved feelings and pay homage to the woman who birthed you into this world. It stimulates self-reflection and gratitude for her relentless efforts and sacrifices. It's an emotionally fulfilling and healing process that can sow seeds of peace, comprehension, and healing. After delving into my personal letter, I encourage you to set aside some quiet moments to write a letter to your mother, or the maternal figure in your life.

Your letter to your mother could be a mixture of emotions – a note of gratitude for her unflinching support, an apology for words unsaid or actions undone, a heartfelt confession of your deepest feelings, or a tribute to her enduring legacy. Whether your mother has been a constant pillar of strength or a complicated figure, this letter can be a cathartic process, bringing to light sentiments you may not have had the opportunity to express before.

Writing this letter is not only a profound demonstration of your love and respect for your mother but also an introspective journey for you. As you pour your thoughts and feelings onto the paper, you may discover parts of yourself - parts shaped and nurtured by her love, or perhaps, tempered by her imperfections.

Use this letter as an opportunity to truly delve into the essence of your relationship with your mother. Let it be an honest reflection of your feelings, be they love, regret, sorrow, or joy. This letter is your chance to express, remember, forgive, and understand. It's an emotional bridge between you and your mother, fostering empathy, healing, and love. So, take your time, embrace the process, and most importantly, write from the heart.

Ma,

Do you know the depth of this void you've left? It's deep, Ma, so deep words aren't enough to describe it. I keep waiting for you to fill it with your laughter, your stories, your love. I find myself in new experiences and opportunities, and all I keep thinking about is sharing them with you.

I can't shake off our last conversation, Ma. It resonates in my mind, reminding me of your pain. It was the worst kind of torment to hear you suffer and know that I couldn't make it better. On that last day, I felt you withdrawing, and I knew it, oh God, I knew, it was our final talk. You were ready to go, you were ready to join Nanny and be with the Lord.

The day God told me to release you, Ma, that was the day my world crumbled. I didn't want to let you go, but I couldn't bear to see you in pain once more. I stopped you when I was 8, but not this time. This time I wasn't going to intervene. I was going to allow you to make your own decision and I was going to be a big boy and support you until the end. So, with a heart that was heavy, full of love, and sorrow, I told you, "Ma, you can rest now. You can go." I bawled, Ma. It hurt like nothing else.

I hope you're not mad at me. I told you that you could go because I didn't want to see you suffer, not to see you go. I wanted you here forever. I battled guilt for a long time, Ma. I wondered if I'd given up on you. I felt lost when I heard about others being visited by you in their dreams. I felt left out. I wondered if you were mad at me for telling you that you can go and rest or not being in New Jersey during your final hours.

Ma, this letter isn't just about that. It's a tribute to you, to everything you've taught me. You, Ma, made me who I am. You taught me kindness, empathy, love, and you even taught me how to fight. You showed me how to take care of myself, you taught me how to put others before me, and how to love unconditionally. Remember how we used to tease you about being nosey? Ma, I'd give anything to hear you one more time.

Your absence is a wound that never heals, eventually, it will. But I carry you with me, in every smile. I share, every helping hand I extend. I remember your smell, and I honor you with every act of kindness. Still, I find myself asking you, begging you, to visit me. I need to know you're okay, that you're proud of me. I wish for a dream, a sign, anything, Mom, to know you're still with me.

Your son Shon,

By the way, your grandson Keymar passed away yesterday while I was writing this letter. I am so sad right now for Billy. He has lost two sons and I can't imagine how he and Michelle feels. But I know God got them and He has all of us. Most importantly I know you're watching over us. Can you tell Javon, TyShon, and Roy that I said hello, and if you happen to see Mr. Knott tell him that I miss him too?

Letter To Your Mother

-7-
DEAR DAD

Our fathers hold a profound place in our hearts, embodying our earliest examples of heroism, our initial templates for adulthood. They lead us into the labyrinth of life, often steering us through the various bends and turns. Yet, the relationships we share with our fathers can sometimes be a complex web of emotions, laden with sentiments unspoken and words unuttered. Crafting a letter to your father can be a transformative journey towards healing and affirmation, a catalyst for change and emotional growth.

It provides an opportunity to appreciate his endeavors and extend your forgiveness for his shortcomings. This simple yet profound act can help repair emotional scars, initiate meaningful conversations, and articulate deep-rooted feelings that may have been lying dormant for years. Writing this letter is more than a simple act of articulating your thoughts and feelings; it is a process of acknowledging and comprehending your father's influence on the canvas of your life.

Moreover, this letter can become a mirror through which you view your past, understand your present, and envision your future. It can help illuminate the man your father was or is and the person you have become because of, or despite, him. You may unearth childhood memories that shaped your identity, moments of wisdom imparted, or confront the harsh realities of wounds left by his actions or absence.

This chapter urges you to take the brave step of penning down these emotions, regardless of the nature of your relationship with your father. It could be a love letter celebrating his dedication, an olive branch extended in the hope of reconciliation, or perhaps a cathartic release of pain and disappointment. Whatever it is, let it be a testament of truth, sincerity, and hope.

In the quiet communion between you and the page, may you discover the courage to bare your heart, the strength to forgive, and the grace to move forward. You are not just writing a letter; you are embarking on a journey of self-discovery and understanding, of love and forgiveness, of healing and growth. Write with honesty, write with love, and most importantly, write for yourself.

Dear Dad,

It's taken me a while to find the right words, to sift through the emotions, to make sense of the past and the present. But here I am, writing to you with a heart that's healed, with a spirit that's stronger, and with a love that's deeper.

I want you to know, first and foremost, that I forgive you. Our past may be marred by misunderstandings and miscommunications, and our bond may have once been strained, but today, I see you for who you truly are - a man who did his best with the tools he had. And you know what, Dad? Your best was more than enough.

I've come to appreciate the father you were, the father you've become. It's true that our relationship was once turbulent, like a boat tossed around in a storm. There were moments when I wanted to scream out in frustration, moments when I was dismissive, abrupt, and even downright rude but I knew you weren't going for that. As a grown man, you still had my respect. Especially after you punked me in front of my wife and kids. They still bring that moment up whenever they feel like bringing me back down to size. I now realize that much of my behavior was rooted in unresolved trauma, in trying to even the score for perceived slights. For all of those moments, I want to say, I'm sorry. Truly, deeply sorry.

The transformation of our relationship has been nothing short of miraculous, Dad. Once strained, it is now full of understanding and mutual respect. It's like we've transitioned from a black-and-white silent film into a vibrant, colorful, high-definition movie. You've become more than just Nate to me, you're my dad, a title I speak with pride, with joy, and most importantly, with love.

You've shown up for me in ways that I never anticipated, especially in my later years. You've been there, really present and involved, something that I never thought I would experience. I now recognize the silent sacrifices you've made, the quiet strength you've displayed, and the unconditional love you've given. You've been a great Dad, and I am grateful.

Thank you, Dad, for everything - for teaching me resilience, for giving me your unwavering support, and for demonstrating what it truly means to love and forgive. I almost forgot, thank you for driving Derrick and me back to Michigan by yourself and turning back around to make it back for work. You did that thing in less than 24hrs. Our relationship has become one of the most cherished aspects of my life. It's dope, Dad, and I wouldn't have it any other way.

With Love,

Shon

Letter To Your Father

_____

_____

_____

_____

_____

_____

_____

_____

_____

_____

_____

_____

_____

_____

_____

_____

-8-
DEAR SHON

Crafting a letter to your past or present self can be an influential practice in self-empathy and self-kindness. This exercise fosters a deeper connection with the individual you once were, and lets you acknowledge the voyage you've embarked on to evolve into the person you are now. This journey is an invitation to bestow forgiveness for past missteps, extend reassurances amidst current uncertainties, and gently carve a path of compassion for your future development.

It's a unique occasion to honor the tenacity you've shown, acknowledge the battles you've waged, and commemorate the triumphs you've achieved. This introspective act can serve as your compass, leading you towards healing, self-acceptance, and personal growth.

Your letter to your younger or current self can be a profound conversation, a gentle dialogue with the soul. You may start by forgiving the child you were for the mistakes made while navigating life's complex terrain, reassure the adult you are today amidst the tumultuous seas of doubt and fear, and lay the foundation for a compassionate future that celebrates growth and understanding.

As you pen this letter, recognize the invaluable lessons each phase of your life has taught you. Encourage yourself to continue being brave, resilient, and hopeful, and celebrate the victories, no matter how small. Reaffirm your worth, strengths, and potential, and acknowledge your imperfections as integral parts of your unique journey.

In this letter, give yourself permission to let go of the burdens of past regrets and future anxieties. Use this opportunity to tell yourself that it's okay to stumble, to not have all the answers, and to have fears. More importantly, remind your past, present, and future self that you are enough, just as you are.

This act of writing a letter to oneself is an intimate journey of rediscovery and acceptance. Let it be a beacon of self-love and self-appreciation that shines light on your path, guiding you towards an empowered future. So, take your time, be patient, and above all, be kind to yourself.

Dear Shon,

There are times when I look at myself in the mirror and the face that looks back at me is not of the man standing there, but of the boy who once was. And today, as I pen down these words to you, it's not just to the resilient man you've become, but also to the 13-year-old boy who's been carrying his wounds silently, even within the strong, 47-year-old exterior.

First, I want to acknowledge your fear – the fear you felt as a boy. You were afraid to fight, afraid to step into the ring. And you know what? That's okay. Fear is not a sign of weakness; it's a sign of being human, of recognizing danger, and acknowledging vulnerability. You were a child, Shon, and it was okay to be scared.

Secondly, about the NFL dream. Dreams, they morph and evolve as we do, and it's okay if some of them remain unfulfilled. Not making it to the NFL was not a testament to your failure but a signpost guiding you towards another journey, a journey that has led you to impact lives of men and their families in more ways than you could've ever done on a football field.

On the subject of quitting – remember, every ending is a new beginning. You hit the reset button, button that reset has become a source of strength and accountability. In life, we often equate quitting with failing. But sometimes, quitting is not giving up, it's choosing to refocus your focus on something more important or something that aligns with your assignment. I'm so glad that you are now chasing your assignment and dominating your lane, rather than chasing likes, approval of others, and the bag. Shon, you chose yourself, your mental health, and your happiness over everything else. The loss of your business, as devastating as it was, is not a reflection of your worth or capabilities. Businesses fail for a multitude of reasons, many beyond the control of an individual. Although yours failed because of your decision making. Look at it this way, would you be you or have what you have if your business didn't fail? I'll answer it for you, NO! Instead of berating yourself for what happened, use the experience as a steppingstone for your future successes.

I know the wounds of your younger self may still run deep. But what I know about you, you will continue to grow from the inside out to continue to work on you. Shon, the judgments, the losses, they still sting. But, Shon, it's time to put down the weight you've been carrying. It's time to forgive yourself – for your perceived shortcomings, for the goals you didn't achieve, for the times you quit. You are so much more than those moments. You are strength personified, a testament to resilience, and a beacon of hope for many.

Look back with understanding. Look back with compassion. See you through His eyes. That's not just for others, it's for you too. You did the best you could with what you knew at the time. So, it's time to heal the wounds of that young boy and let him know that he turned out just fine. He grew into a man who impacts lives, who brings hope to others, who is a role model for resilience and perseverance.
And to the man you are today, remember this: You are worthy. You are deserving. You are enough. Just as you are.

With love, Shon

-9-
LETTER TO MY WIFE & CHILDREN

Our families form the bedrock of our existence - they act as our fortress, our wellspring of happiness, affection, and contentment. However, we often overlook their significance, leaving a myriad of emotions unvoiced. Drafting a letter to your wife, children, and family members that blessed you presents a unique occasion to voice your most profound sentiments of love, admiration, and thankfulness. It acts as a sincere testament to your affection for them, acknowledging their irreplaceable roles in your life.

This exercise fosters open dialogue, strengthens emotional ties, and serves as an enduring keepsake of your love. Through this gesture, you not only affirm their indispensable place in your life but also craft a physical embodiment of your love that they can hold close to their hearts forever.

Your letter to your family could be a canvas of heartfelt emotions – an intimate tribute to your wife for her unwavering support and love, a proclamation of pride for your children's accomplishments and their individuality, and a token of gratitude for your mother-in-law who has been a blessing in disguise.

Use this letter as an opportunity to celebrate your family's unique journey, highlighting moments of shared joy, trials overcome, and lessons learned together. Express your hopes for the future, reinforce your commitment to their happiness and well-being, and assure them of your unending love and support.

Remember, this is more than just a letter; it's a tangible piece of your heart, a cherished keepsake that they can revisit in times of joy and sadness, uncertainty and celebration. It's an affirmation of your love, a promise of your presence, and a testament to your enduring bonds.

So, take your time, delve deep into your emotions, and let your love for your family guide your words. Use this letter as a mirror reflecting your innermost feelings, a bridge connecting your hearts, and a beacon illuminating the strength and depth of your family bonds. Above all, let it be a heartfelt expression of your love, gratitude, and commitment to your precious family.

To My Beautiful and Precious Leah,

There are not enough words in the world to capture the depth of my love for you, but in this letter, I will try my best. Our 21 years of marriage has been a journey, one of the most beautiful, transformative, and meaningful adventures I have ever embarked on.

I remember the day when I first laid eyes on you. You were fresh out of your 21st birthday at B-Dubs, radiating a light that outshined everyone and everything else in the room. Among the many women there, it was your smile that held my gaze, your elegance that captured my heart, and your persona that enticed my soul. That night, my nervousness threatened to hold me back, but thank God for Armando, Mike, and the shy brother role worked. They urged me to approach you in spite of my fearing rejection. Looking back now, I realize that stepping toward you was the best decision I ever made.

Leah, you have been my rock, my guide, my business, and my life partner in every sense of the word. You've stood by me when the storms raged, and together, we've weathered everything that life and marriage have thrown our way. You saw me at my worst, at my most vulnerable state, and yet, you never made me feel small or less than. Yes, there were moments when I felt insecure, and sometimes your confidence intimidated me. But every time I voiced my feelings, you were there, ready to listen, ready to understand, ready to work through it with me. You always spoke to my potential, and always saw the king in me, even when I couldn't see it myself.

Leah, I want to thank you for the love and respect you showed my mother. Even when times were challenging, you never faltered. You treated her with the same warmth and affection as if she was your own, and for that, I am eternally grateful.

We have had our fair share of trials, of lows that threatened to break us. But even at those moments, we chose love, forgiveness, and seeing each other through His eyes. We chose to see each other for who we truly were, not for the mistakes we've made or the trials we've faced.

Leah, I want you to know, with absolute certainty, that God made you for me and I for you. It is a joy and an honor to call you mine, just as I am yours. Here's to us, to the beautiful family we've created, to the love that binds us, and to the life we've built together. I want you to feel my heart, I want you to know that you are cherished, loved, and celebrated every single day.

All my love,

Shon aka Boochie

Dear Syd My Incredible and Resilient one,

The day you were born, my life took on a new meaning. You were the one who initiated me into fatherhood, who ignited a spark within me to seek my purpose and the best version of myself. I looked into your tiny eyes and knew that I wanted to be your everything. So, I began the work of self-improvement and sought guidance on how to become a better man, a better father.

In the early years of your life, I confess, I made mistakes. I was figuring out how to parent, how to navigate this immense responsibility of raising a child. I regret that I parented you at times out of my own pain and trauma. There were moments when I referred to you as my "practice baby", and I want you to know, despite the lightheartedness of that term, I gave you my all, the best I had, and the best I could give during those times. I ask for your forgiveness for any missteps, or any decisions I made that may have hurt you.

Sydni, as I see the woman you're becoming, my heart swells with pride. You've grown into an extraordinary individual - compassionate, resilient, and determined. The meaning we assigned to your name manifests itself in you every single day; you are the epitome of it. I want you to know that I strive every day to express my love for you in ways that resonate with you and to support you in the ways you need. I know that I don't hit the ball out the park at every at-bat, but I will keep swinging for the fences. I will never ever stop swinging for you. You're my oldest child, the one who made me a father, and you hold a unique place in my heart.

Looking ahead, I know you will touch the lives of those around you in incredible ways. I have no doubt that you will be a wonderful mother and an amazing wife. The man who wins your heart will indeed have found a priceless treasure and gem.

Please know that I am, and will always be, here for you. And above all, always remember how very much I love you.

With all my heart,

Daddy

My Sweet Shelby,

From the moment you entered our world, you made it easy for us to shower you with our love. You've always had this special ability, a kind of superpower, to warm our hearts and make us smile, even in the toughest of times your spirit makes everything better. As you grow, that hasn't changed about you.

As your father, I see so much of myself reflected in you. But even more than that, I see a beautiful intelligent, compassionate, and deeply sensitive young woman who continues to surprise and delight me every day. Shelby, the sound of your laugh is a breath of fresh air. It's a melody that I love to hear. Let no person, no situation, or no devil in hell steal that joy from you. Keep laughing baby, keep that laughter alive, Laugh, baby, laugh!

You have a passion and taste for life that inspires me to keep working hard on my journey. It's no secret that your taste leans towards the finer things, and I wouldn't want it any other way. I have to admit, it gives me motivation to keep going after my dreams because I want to be able to provide you with the desires of your heart.

Every time you hug me, every time you hit me playfully, I'm reminded of how much you love me. Your love is a blessing to me, a gift that I'll cherish each day. Shelby, you are extremely gifted and talented, and I pray that you realize the full extent of your potential. There's a world within you waiting to be discovered, a wealth of abilities that can only be unlocked by you and take you anywhere you want to go.

I often tell you, half-jokingly, that you must be a boss or marry rich because of your desire for the 'soft life' as your momma describes it. But in all seriousness, I want you to have a life of ease, a life that is as beautiful and as wonderful as you are.

And whatever path you choose, I want you to know that I will always be here for you, cheering you on, providing a shoulder to lean on when you need it, and celebrating every single one of your accomplishments. You are a blessing to me, Shelby, and I love you more than words can express.

Always,

Daddy

Dear Levi,

From the moment I found out I was going to have a son, my heart swelled with pride and joy. It wasn't just the thought of having a son, but the prospect of sharing my legacy with someone who would carry it forward. Now, every day I look at you, I see that legacy come to life, and I'm more grateful than ever. I wouldn't have it any other way, and I can't think of a better person to continue the legacy we're creating together.

I see in you a strength, a resilience, and a confidence that far exceed what I had at your age. You possess a powerful spirit that leaves an indelible impression on everyone you encounter. There's an unshakeable belief in yourself that fuels you, and I admire that deeply. Never let anyone mistake that self-belief for arrogance. You know who you are, and that's an incredible gift.

Levi, you demonstrate a deep level of compassion and consideration for those around you, particularly your sisters and your mother. I see how you make decisions, taking into account their feelings and well-being. It's a mark of your character and a testament to the kind of man you're becoming.

I watch you observing me, and I know you're learning from how I treat your mother and your sisters. Your respect and your regard for women speak volumes about your character. I have no doubt that you will treat all women with the respect, kindness, and honor they deserve. You're already showing signs of being a better man than I ever was. In you, I see limitless potential. I have no doubt that you will achieve any and everything you set your heart and mind to. Your ambition and drive are truly inspiring.

I want you to remember always to keep Christ at the center of your life. His love and guidance have been the cornerstone of our lives, and it's my hope that they will continue to be for you.

And finally, I want you to know how proud I am to be your father. I am not just proud; I am humbled and grateful for the opportunity to witness your journey. You inspire me every day, and I can't wait to see the amazing things you will do in your life.

With all my love,

Daddy

Dear Moms,

I'm writing this letter to you with a heart filled with love, admiration, and deep gratitude for you. These simple words can never truly encapsulate all that you mean to me, but I hope they offer a glimpse of my profound respect and love for you.

During challenging chapters in my life, you have been a beacon of unwavering support, illuminating my path with your strength, wisdom, and faith. Your prayers enveloped me in comfort and guided me through the darkest of times. It's a testament to your incredible spirit, and for that, I am eternally grateful.

You were the first to discern God's calling in my life, recognizing the divine purpose that has since become my guiding light. Your faith in me, even when I struggled to believe in myself, has been a significant source of my strength. Your love and faith in God's plans for me have been a steady anchor, inspiring me to follow this divine path.

I can still feel the warmth of the love you showered upon my mother before her passing. You loved her, supported her, and stood by her with a grace that I will forever remember. This act of love, amongst many others, is a testament to the beautiful soul you possess.

Your strength and resilience, especially after the profound loss of your beloved husband and daughter, have left me in awe. These trials would have broken many, but you, Moms, have stood unwavering, showcasing a strength that is both inspiring and humbling. I am incredibly proud of you and am honored to be a part of your life.

It is a blessing to be able to call you my mother-in-law, and even more so to regard you as a friend and guide. You have been an incredible mother not just to your children, but to me as well. You've embraced me as your own, and for that, I am eternally thankful. Moreover, the love, wisdom, and guidance you've bestowed upon your grandchildren have left an indelible mark on their hearts, shaping them into the wonderful individuals they are growing to be.

I want you to know how much I love you and appreciate your presence in my life. Your guidance, support, and boundless love have enriched my life in more ways than I can express.

I am blessed to have you in my life, Moms.

Letter To Your Family

-10-
UNbroken

Becoming unbroken is a hard journey and far from a walk in the park. It's not about whether you can do it or not, it's about sticking to it long after the initial motivation to become unbroken has faded away due to continual internal and external struggles. Once you take a stand, once you decide you're gonna put in the work to become unbroken, life's gonna test you. You'll come face-to-face with reminders of your past hurt, people who did you wrong might not show a hint of regret, especially the way you expect them to. But that's where the real work begins. The work of, how do you move forward if the person who hurt you denies their role in your offense or refuses to take responsibility.

During such circumstances, the real question you need to ask yourself is this: will I remain dedicated to the pursuit of becoming unbroken even when they don't take responsibility? Becoming unbroken doesn't follow a linear path, and it doesn't travel down a smooth road, but the journey is part of the healing process.

Let's look at it this way. Imagine your life as a garden, a place where beautiful flowers and pesky weeds coexist. The flowers represent the best parts of you - your dreams, your strengths, your values, the love you have to give. The weeds? They symbolize the challenges, traumas, heartbreaks, and disappointments that have tried to choke out your growth. This journey of becoming unbroken is much like the tug of war-that takes place in this garden.

On one hand, you've got these vibrant, colorful flowers that reflect the best parts of who you are and what you aspire to be. They're rooted deep within you, constantly reaching for the sun, striving for growth, and flourishing against the odds. On the other hand, the weeds of past hurt, fear, and regret are always trying to invade, spreading their roots and striving to overshadow the flowers.

Here's the thing, though. Both the flowers and the weeds are a part of your garden, your life. They are integral to your growth. Yes, even the weeds. They represent the trials and tribulations you've gone through, the battles you've fought, and the lessons you've learned. They remind you of where you've been, but more importantly, they show you how strong you can be.

The key to transforming from broken to unbroken is understanding this - you've got to tend to your garden, pull out those weeds of self-doubt, fear, and regret, and make room for your flowers to bloom. This journey isn't about denying the existence of the weeds. It's about acknowledging them, understanding their purpose, and learning to manage them so they don't overrun your garden.

Just as you wouldn't condemn a garden for having weeds, don't condemn yourself for carrying past hurts. They're a part of your journey, but they don't define you. It's the flowers that you nurture and the garden you cultivate from those experiences that truly tell your story of becoming unbroken.

147

The journey from 'Broken Boys' to 'Unbroken Men' is a deeply personal journey that often starts in the heart where the burden of painful memories and unresolved trauma resides. Yet, the hardest part of this journey is usually the very beginning. It's the stage where you grapple with the decision to grant forgiveness to someone you've deemed unforgivable, and that someone can include yourself.

While both steps are tough, it was self-forgiveness that posed the most intimidating obstacle for me. To some extent, I was prepared to relinquish the person who hurt me of their burden. However, when it came to forgiving myself, I was resistant. I felt undeserving of forgiveness and grace, primarily because of the perceived disgrace I brought upon my family by having to experience a failed business venture that led to having to file bankruptcy.

I tried to mask my issues, my worries as concern for my family, but in reality, it was all about me. My mind was racing with questions: How will people perceive me? How were my old teammates gonna see me? Were they whispering behind my back, "Man, he couldn't cut it in football, now look at him, flunking out in business too?" How would my church family view me? I was a success story, a tither, generously planting financial seeds in people's lives, spreading the good word with sincerity and heart, and now here I am, navigating the rough waters of a business gone under.

Like I said, I tried to play it off like my worry was all about the image of my family, but the truth was, it was my image I was concerned about. Will I still have the respect of my peers and others? The weight of shame, that was all on me. I'd dreamt all my life of making it to the

NFL, buying my mom a big, beautiful house, my dad a shiny new car, and setting my family up financially for the rest of their lives. So, having a prospering clothing store where I was selling and shipping products to NBA and NFL players alike, was my crescendo, my touchdown, my own spin on reaching the NFL.

I was left standing there grappling with the ghost of trauma that reared its ugly head again. The feeling of being too small, hitting that darn reset button, was all too familiar. I suppose I thought launching a clothing store would fill that void and would be a solid replacement for self-fulfillment. Boy, was I selling myself a pack of lies!

Yet, it was a façade, it was me wearing the "Lion Mask". The sense of accomplishment it brought was short-lived and superficial. I walked around with my head held high, thinking my achievements would keep the feelings of insignificance at bay. But with a poverty, aka "stinking thinking' mentality deeply ingrained in me and a lack of self-belief, I was always waiting for the bottom to fall out. My fear had me only playing defense, rather than playing all phases of the game. Which ultimately lead to my business's failure. I kept hearing the voice of my father, "You're too small."

From the outside looking in, people saw a confident, and determined man, a hustler that was bound to make his mark in this world. Yet, when I had to close down my shop, a deep, long-buried wound was ripped open again. Suddenly, I felt insignificant and small again. Almost as if I was back to being that boy who needed his cousin to fight his battles. I had to start on the grueling path of forgiving myself for the financial burden I'd put my family under and for the fallout of bankruptcy.

But let me tell you, even in the midst of such adversity,

something beautiful sprouted. This crisis became a catalyst for growth, solidifying the bond between my wife and I. Listen ya'll, she NEVER blamed me, never used the situation as a weapon to cut me down or emasculate me. And trust me, she could have. Now, I'm not saying she didn't blame me, or even say I told you so in her head or to her friends. I… don't… know… But what I do know, she never openly, said it to me personally or made me feel like she was disappointed and could no longer follow me as a husband and as a leader of our home. We've all seen those couples, right? The ones who wait for the perfect storm to hit their partnership right where it hurts. But not Leah. She knew I was already drowning in guilt and suffocated by regret. My ego and my misguided thought processes had stood in the way of me being a strong leader.

So, owning up to my mistakes, and taking responsibility, was a crucial first step in the right direction. But living with the remorse of putting my family in a difficult situation, made self-forgiveness tough. Funny, isn't it, how often we find it easier to forgive others but struggle when it comes to ourselves? That's because we're quick to judge our actions, but slower on judging our intentions. On the flip side, we tend to judge others by their intentions and give less weight to their actions. We're ready to give them room to learn and grow, but when it comes to ourselves, we're all about "get over it" and "man up!" However, this is also true in the case when men do not take personal responsibility and accountability. The same concept is applied but in reverse. We would judge ourselves by our intentions rather than actions when we want to hold others accountable and not ourselves. So, I challenge you to take a good look at yourself and see where you are when it comes to personal and external forgiveness.

Eventually, not only did I manage to forgive myself, but I also began to share my experiences, my struggles, and my lessons learned, hoping they could serve as a bridge or blueprint for other men's journey to becoming UNbroken. As I embarked on this journey of sharing and healing, I was confronted with another profound challenge that required me to dig deeper into my emotional reservoir. The thought of freeing those who had hurt me both emotionally and mentally was nearly insurmountable. I believed they should face damning consequences to experience a taste of the agony they had imposed upon me. My trauma and fury longed for revenge, or any sign of remorse, a semblance of regret, an indication that they were genuinely repentant. But to be completely honest, no matter what they did or said in an attempt to ease my suffering, it was going to always fall short. Nothing was ever sufficient. It was as though I had created an impossible expectation, a threshold so towering that no expression of remorse or humility could possibly satisfy my hunger for getting even. In fact, I found myself angry at God when the healing began to take place within me. Letting go of my grudges was a struggle. I found myself actively seeking pain and justifications to refuel my anger. The seeming injustice of it all was that I was the one suffering from sleepless nights, anxiety, depression, fear, and worry, while they seemed to get off scot-free, that was straight-up overwhelming. Letting go was clearly the healthier choice, but I had convinced myself that they deserved to endure the consequences of their actions. Clearly this mindset had me blinded and would not allow me to see past my own pain to heal.

As I continued my journey, I began to understand that the true power in forgiveness was having the power to heal and become unbroken, it is part of the self-healing process. It wasn't about receiving an apology or getting even. At the end of the day, it was all about me healing me. and knowing that it was part of my own healing process, an essential step towards my path of personal restoration with those who hurt me.

The transformational journey from a broken boy to an unbroken man is like the process of Kintsugi. If you are unaware of Kintsugi, let me paint you a picture. It's an ancient art form that originated in Japan, where they take broken pottery and instead of tossing it aside or putting it in the garbage, they piece it back together. Now here's the kicker - they don't just glue it back together and hope nobody notices the cracks. No, they take gold, or sometimes silver or platinum, and they use the precious metals to seal up the fractures.

Kintsugi is all about honoring the breakage, the very cracks that once signified destruction. They showcase the beauty in the flaws, turning what was once a point of weakness into a bold declaration of strength. Instead of hiding the cracks, they're highlighted. Glorified even. And what you end up with isn't just a mended piece of pottery, but a symbol of resilience, of overcoming, of transformation. It's no longer just a pot or a cup or a vase. It's a story of survival, of healing, of becoming unbroken. That's Kintsugi. It's about accepting the brokenness of our past, finding the strength and beauty within those cracks and using it to create a new narrative. And guess what? We can apply this same philosophy to our own lives. Each of us can turn our wounds into wisdom, our fractures into strength, and our scars into stories of survival. That's what becoming unbroken is all about.

It's not our past hurts or mistakes, but the act of healing them that brings out our inner strength and wisdom. Each golden seam of repair stands as a testament to resilience, a beacon of hope signaling the promise of a better, stronger future. That's the heart of becoming unbroken – taking our past pains and transforming them into a powerful story of survival and personal growth.

Now, here's the real challenge for many of us men in our journey towards becoming unbroken: we're often too caught up in this internal war, torn between what was and what lies ahead. We don't cut ourselves much slack, and that's in no small part due to what society has been feeding us about what it means to be a man.

To truly become unbroken, we've got to stand up against and address these stereotypes head-on – that we always need to suppress our emotions, that our worth is measured by our sexual conquests, that we're supposed to silently deal with our mental health, that we need to resort to physical aggression to solve our problems. We've been sold this narrative that aggression is the solution, but the truth is, aggression only buries our traumas deeper, delaying the healing. It's time to flip the script.

To start looking at our wounds as trauma, to begin the healing, we've got to first be willing to dig deep and let go of control. We have to embrace vulnerability. As men, we're trained to be stoic, stern, and straightforward, and to scrutinize our flaws and failures with a lens of judgment, and resentment. Rarely do we get to see grace playing its part in our lives.

Now, if we want to become truly unbroken, we've got to unlearn these toxic teachings. Now, I know you're not going to be able to unlearn what you already know. It's more about shifting your belief system by gaining more insight and information to give yourself options and opportunities to grow mentally and emotionally. We've got to start seeing ourselves not as isolated, invulnerable entities, but as human beings capable of grace, forgiveness, and emotional growth. That's the way forward, my brothers. That's how we break these chains and become unbroken.

When you look at the story of Mephibosheth, 1 Samuel 4:4 it offers a great depiction of this transformation. Mephibosheth was not born broken, he became broken. He became handicapped due to an accident that was no fault of his own. If you are unfamiliar with the story, Mephibosheth's journey began with a tragic incident during his childhood. As a young child, he suffered a debilitating fall that left him crippled.

This unfortunate event happened while his nanny, driven by fear and desperation, was attempting to evade an imminent threat from an advancing army. She was carrying him in her arms when he was dropped, leaving him impaired for life. And here's where I want to invite you to shift your perspective - instead of focusing on what's wrong with you, consider what happened to you. Many of you may have experienced sexual assault, witnessed your parents' divorce, faced bullying, been born with a handicap, lived in poverty, or endured physical and emotional trauma. You've journeyed through life without ever addressing these traumatic events and their aftermath - it's not your fault that someone dropped you. You have to understand that many of our life issues surrounding trauma were no fault of our own. Perhaps you were forced into the role of being the 'man of the house' at a very young age because your parents were battling drug addiction, or you had to step up to help your single mother make ends meet.

Whatever your circumstances were that contributed to your adult trauma, I want you to examine them in the light of Mephibosheth's story and the art form of Kintsugi. This isn't about pinpointing what's wrong with you - it's about understanding what happened to you. Events that were out of your control are not your fault, and you need to extend yourself some grace. When we apply the philosophy of Kintsugi to our lives, we understand how our scars have shaped us into who we are today. They enhance our beauty. You shouldn't have to bear the weight of your childhood trauma, especially when it was beyond your control.

However, for those who have made bad decisions that led to self-inflicted wounds or caused trauma to others, while I don't want to seem dismissive, it's critical that you extend grace towards yourself too. Accept accountability and responsibility for your actions, but don't condemn yourself to a life sentence of regret, self-pity, or perpetual suffering.

Remember Mephibosheth. Despite his trauma and self-perceived lack of value, his story didn't end with his trauma. The same applies to you - your past does not dictate your future. Your story doesn't end with your trauma either.

Despite his physical limitations, Mephibosheth's found grace in his brokenness, a grace that was extended to him by King David. He was given a place at the King's table, not as a servant, but as a son. This signified not just acceptance, but an assertion of his worth and identity despite his brokenness. You don't have to wait for a David to come along and offer you a seat at the table, you can either invite people to your table, eat at your own table, or finally create your own table if it doesn't exist. The bottom line is, you're responsible for your own healing and you can't wait for others to apologize or acknowledge their wrongdoings against you.

Mephibosheth's narrative is a lesson that even though we might be broken in places that seems to be beyond repair, it's never too fragmented to pick up the pieces and start the process of becoming unbroken. It's not about assigning blame, not on yourself, not on others, or even on your past. What counts is how you rise, how you harness the shattered pieces of your past and use them as steppingstones towards becoming unbroken. I urge you to perceive your brokenness not as a burden, but as a source of unmatched strength. Let it instill in you a sense of humility and empathy - these are the bedrocks upon which you can build your unbroken self.

Mephibosheth's story resonates with many of us. Why and how? Because he wasn't born broken, he became broken. Life dealt him a difficult hand through someone else's actions. The very hands that were supposed to shield him ended up dropping him, altering his life's course. You too might find echoes of your own journey in his story. Figuratively, you may have also been dropped, unexpectedly shifting from an active, 'normal' life to a sedentary existence.

As Mephibosheth possibly struggled to come to terms with his drastically changed circumstances, we are left to wonder, did he have someone help him navigate his storm of emotions and feelings? Better yet, who helped you navigate yours? I will pause right there. I want that to sink in. Are you battling or currently struggling because someone dropped you and refused to do what was necessary to help you grow from the inside out?

When life shatters us like pottery, it's not the end of the road. It's quite the opposite. It's an opportunity to rebuild, to create something even more extraordinary. Each fracture filled with gold, is a testament to our journey, our resilience.

My personal journey toward becoming unbroken meant that I had to face my pain, not run from it. I had to dig deep, look into the darkest corners of my heart and confront the wounds that had been festering for far too long. It was only by shining a light on the pain I harbored that I began to heal and grow. Becoming unbroken isn't about erasing or forgetting our past. It's about accepting our past, learning from our pain, and using it as a catalyst for growth and transformation.

See, becoming unbroken is about reconciliation with our past, and harnessing it to construct a stronger, resilient future. Your brokenness isn't your weakness; it's your strength. It's the map that has charted your journey so far and will guide you on the path toward becoming unbroken.

While I yearned for my father to express sorrow, remorse, and repentance, I realized that would have been nice, but not necessary. It really wasn't and isn't about him apologizing after all these years. It is and always really all about me, my journey, and my healing. This isn't about pointing fingers; it's about looking inward and assessing our own actions and reactions. It's about healing the wounds that we've been carrying and becoming a better version of ourselves.

There were tendencies within me I had to confront - my habit of backing down when the going got tough, a pattern that took root when I was merely 10. It's something I never really addressed or grappled with until I chose to be deliberate about my healing to become unbroken.

I had to be generous with grace, especially towards my younger self, the 13-year-old boy I scorned for being too scared to fight back. The 13-year-old boy that gave his daughter advice about conflict resolution. The boy who needed his female cousin to step in and rescue him. In my journey to becoming unbroken, I had to come to terms with my past actions, choices, and decisions. I had to address my internal narrative - the stories I had been telling myself, the stories that held me captive. These were stories of fear, inadequacy, and regret, all of which had been woven into the fabric of my identity over the years. But, to become unbroken, I had to acknowledge that I am not the sum of my past failures or missteps. Instead, I am the resilience that keeps me standing, the courage that propels me forward, and the wisdom that emerges from every wound healed. I am a testament to the possibility of transformation, a living proof that brokenness can birth strength, that pain can fuel purpose.

As we, you and I continue to walk this journey, we must also understand that we are not alone. Every father that has ever entered my programming at InvolvedDad has always thought that they were alone until they realized that they weren't. My friend, you're not alone and you will never be alone.

In the end, the journey of becoming unbroken is not simply about mending our wounds, but rather about unearthing our genuine identities. It's about navigating the depths of our souls to find our inner peace, fortitude, our capacity to endure adversity, and our ability to both give and receive love, despite the scars we bear. We've come to understand that it's not about concealing our fractures, but rather about embracing them as a part of who we are, a testament to the trials we've weathered and the strength we've discovered within ourselves.

As we conclude this chapter, remember that each step you take on this journey is a step toward healing, growth, and transformation. At one time you were defined and shaped by your brokenness, but I declare that today you are defined by your resilience and your ability to rise from the ashes. You are more than your pain. You are more than your past. You are unbroken. And your journey continues...

-BONUS-
UNBROKEN: EMBARKING ON YOUR NEW BEGINNING

As we journey to the end of this book, it's important to realize that in truth, we are arriving at a new beginning - YOUR new beginning. This book isn't just about my story; it's also a testament to the unbroken spirit within each one of us, waiting to break free and fulfill its true destiny.

Throughout this journey, you've seen me revisit the painful past, the heartaches, the setbacks, and you've seen me embrace forgiveness, self-love, and purpose. Now, it's your turn. It's time for you to pen your own narrative, your own 'unbroken' story.

This chapter is about you - your resilience, your strength, and your potential for an unbroken life that is aligned with your purpose. But remember, it starts with a commitment. A commitment to introspection, to healing, to growing, and to emerging out of the shadows of brokenness.

You're about to embark on a path towards your new beginning, a path that leads you to the most authentic version of yourself. A self that is unbroken, fulfilled, and on a mission to achieve its life's purpose and destiny. It's a path only you can carve out and a story only you can tell.

And that story needs to be written. By you.

In the coming pages, you will find blank space - consider this as your canvas. Reflect on your experiences, your dreams, your aspirations, and start crafting your new narrative. Write about your journey, your healing, your growth. Write about your commitment to an unbroken life, to fulfilling your purpose, and about the first steps you're taking on this new path.

The power of writing your own narrative is profound. It's cathartic, healing, and empowering. So, pick up that pen, and begin writing your own chapter of unbroken resilience and new beginnings.

You're not merely a reader of this story anymore; you're the author of your own. It's your turn to document your journey towards a fulfilling life, a life where brokenness no longer holds the reins. It's your turn to inspire the world with your narrative of hope, strength, resilience, and an unbroken spirit.

Remember, your story is unique, your journey is your own, and only you can tell it as it is. Here's to a new beginning, to a life of purpose, to a life unbroken. It's your story. Write it well. And remember, you are not alone. You have the power to create your own destiny, and in doing so, you will light the way for others to do the same. Now, go forth and tell the world your story.

Write your new beginning.

Your Story:

ABOUT THE AUTHOR

Shon Hart is a man on a mission to change lives, one father at a time. His own journey from challenging beginnings to becoming a dedicated advocate for engaged fatherhood has given him a unique perspective on the transformative power of personal growth and service.

Originally from New Jersey, Shon moved to Michigan in 1993 to play football at Michigan State University. He quickly became a Spartan in spirit, earning an athletic scholarship. His years as a student-athlete taught him valuable lessons in teamwork, leadership, and resilience that he carries into his life and work today.

After graduation, Shon found his life's calling. Now, he's not only a devoted husband to his wife, Leah, and a proud father to Sydni, Shelby, and Levi, but he's also a beacon of hope for many fathers in his community. He lives his values, setting an example of committed parenting and healthy familial relationships that echo his professional pursuits.

Shon is the heart and mind behind InvolvedDad, a non-profit organization designed to champion the cause of fatherhood involvement and foster strong family bonds. He has been instrumental in launching several impactful programs through InvolvedDad, helping countless families in the Flint area and creating lasting change.

A charismatic speaker, Shon has graced numerous platforms with his inspiring talks on active fatherhood. He hosts workshops and training sessions, using his own experiences as a launchpad to ignite the spark of transformation in others.

Grounded in his faith, Shon's approach to life and work reflects a deep spirituality. He has harnessed the power of change, forgiveness, and personal growth, weaving these elements into his daily life and his work with InvolvedDad.

Made in the USA
Middletown, DE
07 November 2023

42098476R00106